Capital & Production

Richard von Strigl

Translated from the German by
Margaret Rudelich Hoppe and
Hans-Hermann Hoppe

Edited with an Introduction
by Jörg Guido Hülsmann

Copyright 2000 by The Ludwig von Mises Institute.

Index prepared by Richard Perry.

Published by The Ludwig von Mises Institute, 518 West Magnolia Avenue, Auburn, Alabama 36832-4528.

Kapital und Produktion copyright 1934 by Julius Springer, Vienna. Printed in Austria.

Capital & Production is an English translation of the above work.

Large Print Edition published 2012 by Skyler J. Collins.
Visit: www.skylerjcollins.com

Cover image by StockFreeImages.com.

ISBN-13: 978-1479321698
ISBN-10: 1479321699

Contents

Introduction (Jörg Guido Hülsmann)...vii
Foreword (Richard von Strigl)..xxix

Chapter 1
Capitalist Production
  1. Factors of Production...1
  2. Roundabout Production...2
  3. The Length of Roundabout Production.............................6
  4. Relatively Durable Factors of Production.......................14
  5. Forms of Capital...26

Chapter 2
The Vertical and Horizontal Connectivity of Prices
  1. The Price System..37
  2. The Supply of Factors of Production..............................39
  3. The Supply and Demand of Entrepreneurs.
     The Law of Costs..43
  4. Complementary Factors of Production. The "Law
     of Diminishing Returns" and the Principle of
     Marginal Productivity...46
  5. Capital Interest and the Temporal Regulation of
     the Structure of Production..52
  6. The Supply of Capital..61
  7. The Prices of Original Factors of Production
     in Capitalist Production..65
  8. The Principle of Substitution and the Horizontal
     Connectivity of Prices...76
  9. Marginal Productivity and the Formation of Costs.
     The Static System...79

Chapter 3
Money and Capital
  1. Price System and Price Level..91
  2. Capital in the Form of Money Assets.............................94
  3. Credit and Money Interest..109
  4. Production Under the Impact of a Credit
     Expansion...120

v

Appendix I
On the Problem of Business Cycles
    1. Prenote..135
    2. The Two Turning Points in the Business Cycle................137
    3. Is the Recurrence of Crises Necessary?
        The Problem of Trade Cycle Policy..........................151
    4. How to Explain the Business Cycle....................................158

Appendix II
A Postscript on the Concept of Capital...161

Literature..165

Index..169

INTRODUCTION

I

The 1920s and 1930s were a glorious era in the history of the Austrian School of economics. In those days, the city of Vienna saw the first genuine culture of scholars working in the tradition established by Carl Menger, and this culture radiated throughout the rest of the German-speaking world and into other countries.

Many important works of this period have been translated into English, in particular, the books by Ludwig von Mises and F.A. Hayek, and also works of other scholars like Fritz Machlup, Gottfried von Haberler, Oskar Morgenstern, Franz Čuhel, Hans Mayer, Paul Rosenstein-Rodan, and Leo Schönfeld-Illy.[1]

Among the pioneering works of this time that have hitherto not been accessible to the anglophone public is that by Richard von Strigl. First published in 1934 under the title *Kapital und Produktion* by the former Austrian Institute for Business Cycle Research in its series "Contributions to Business Cycle Research,"[2] it was reprinted in 1982 by Philosophia Verlag in

---

[1]For a sample of writings by these authors from the inter-war period see *Austrian Economics: A Sampling in the History of a Tradition*, Israel M. Kirzner, ed., vol. 2 (London: William Pickering, 1994).

[2]*Beiträge zur Konjunkturforschung*, edited by the Österreichischen Institut für Konjunkturforschung. The first seven volumes in this series are all classics of Austrian economics: F.A. Hayek, *Geldtheorie und Konjunkturtheorie* (Vienna: Hölder-Pichler-Tempsky, 1929); Fritz Machlup, *Börsenkredit, Industriekredit und Kapitalbildung* (Vienna: Springer, 1931); F.A. Hayek, *Preise und Produktion* (Vienna: Springer, 1933); Erich Schiff, *Kapitalbildung und Kapitalaufzehrung im Konjunkturverlauf* (Vienna: Springer, 1933); Oskar Morgenstern, *Die Grenzen der Wirtschaftspolitik* (Vienna: Springer, 1934); Fritz Machlup, *Führer durch die Krisenpolitik* (Vienna: Manz, [1934] 1998); and Richard von Strigl, *Kapital und Produktion* (Munich:

Munich under the editorship of Professor Barry Smith. The English translation is due to the efforts of Professor Hans-Hermann and Mrs. Margaret Hoppe, and has been made possible by a gift to the Mises Institute by Dr. Mark Skousen. It has been distributed for some time as a typewritten manuscript and is only now being published as a book complete with an index.

In *Capital and Production*, Strigl seeks to come to grips with the causes and possible cures for the Great Depression that plagued the Western world in the aftermath of 1929. Although many other Austrian economists of the time were engaged in similar projects, Strigl's work stands out for its analysis of time-consuming roundabout production processes and of their relevance for the Great Depression.[3] This is what makes the book relevant again at the beginning of the twenty-first century, at a moment of history marked by the most extraordinary global bull market the world has ever experienced.

Strigl combined Jevons's and Böhm-Bawerk's theory of capital into a genuinely Austrian theory of the economy as a whole; and he carefully analyzed the impact of credit expansion on the workings of this macroeconomy. His treatment of these issues is even more systematic, rigorous, and clear than the well-known works by Hayek which covered the same ground. In fact, Hayek hailed Strigl's work "for the simplicity and clarity of exposition of a notoriously difficult subject."[4]

Capital and Production is therefore not merely of interest for historians of thought. Rather it is a yet-to-be-discovered treasure trove for modern economists who seek to develop capital-based macroeconomics. Strigl's ideas will enrich the current literature in this

---

Philosophia, [1934] 1982). After Mises's departure from Vienna in 1934, Morgenstern, who in 1931 had succeeded Hayek as the director of the Institute, set out to publish works with a markedly less Austrian orientation. See for example volume eight in the series, Ragnar Nurske, *Internationale Kapitalbewegungen* (Vienna: Springer, 1935).

[3]Other important contemporary works in this field were Mises's booklet *Die Ursachen der Wirtschaftskrise* (Tübingen: Mohr, 1931); Hayek's *Prices and Production*, 2nd ed. (London: Macmillan, [1931] 1935); and Lionel Robbins's *The Great Depression* (Plainview, N.Y.: Books for Libraries Press, [1934] 1976).

[4]F.A. Hayek, "Richard von Strigl," *Economic Journal* 54:285 (1943).

field and chances are actually high that they will have a greater success now than in the 1930s when the language barrier, political circumstances, and the general intellectual climate prevented them from having any major impact on economists and the public.[5]

Not all readers will be entirely satisfied with Strigl's analysis of the impact of money on the economy. But they will come to appreciate Strigl as a great pioneer of capital-based macroeconomics whose ideas have particular relevance in the present context.

II

Like many other luminaries of pre-World War II Austrian intellectual and artistic life, Richard Ritter von Strigl was a native of former Moravia (which is today a part of the Czech Republic) where he was born February 7, 1891. He studied at the University of Vienna and was admitted as a very young man to the famous private seminar of Eugen von Böhm-Bawerk, which had produced a whole generation of promising economists, such as Otto Bauer, Nicolai Bukharin, Ludwig von Mises, Otto Neurath, and Joseph Schumpeter.

After World War I, Strigl continued his research and wrote an important book on economic theory for which, in 1923, he received his Habilitation—the traditional professors' diploma of the universities of Central Europe. Five years later he acceded to the rank of titular extraordinary professor. However, like Mises, Machlup, Haberler, and other great Viennese economists of the time, he had to earn his living largely outside of academia, eventually becoming a high official at the Austrian Unemployment Insurance Board.

Strigl was a modest, humane, cultured, and very bright man who impressed both his students and impartial colleagues. As one of his pupils, Joseph Steindl stated after his death, "There were few of his pupils or of the foreign economists who would

---

[5]For contemporary works in capital-based macroeconomics, see Mark Skousen, *The Structure of Production* (New York: New York University Press, 1990) and Roger Garrison, *Time and Money* (London: Routledge, 2000). A good modern discussion of capital theory is also in Peter Lewin, *Capital in Disequilibrium* (London: Routledge, 1999).

visit Vienna and sojourn in his circle of those days who did not very much like him."[6] He also had extraordinary gifts for systematic exposition and step-by-step argument, which made for great success in the classroom. Due to these personal and intellectual talents, Strigl had a considerable influence on the generation of young economists graduating from the University of Vienna after World War I. More than any other teacher he shaped the minds of Hayek, Haberler, Machlup, Morgenstern, and other future great Viennese economists.[7]

Strigl convinced his students that economic theory could be studied in its own right, that is, without engaging in previous empirical field studies. And this theory could be used both to explain economic phenomena and to direct political action. Today these views are fairly widespread if not yet part of mainstream economics. However, in the interwar period, matters were very different.

Despite the flourishing of Austrian economics in the 1920s and 1930s, the dominating intellectual force in the economics departments of Germany and Austria was the so-called Historical School. The representatives of this school of thought despised economic theory for its advocacy of universally valid economic laws. They argued that laws could only be as universal as the conditions to which they referred. Since history was a process of constant transformation of the conditions of human existence, there could be no such thing as general economic law. At best, there could only be "laws" describing the economy of a more or less unique period and, at any rate, all insights about this economy had to be derived from studies of concrete households, firms, administrations, towns, etc.

Moreover, Strigl's department at the University of Vienna was a stronghold of antirationalist "organic" economics. The most important advocates of this doctrine were Othmar Spann

---

[6]As quoted in Hayek, "Richard von Strigl," pp. 284–86.

[7]According to Hayek, "Richard von Strigl," p. 284, these young economists "owed more to him than to any other teacher." See also Joseph Steindl as quoted in ibid. and Steindl, "Strigl, Richard von (1891–1942)," in *The New Palgrave: A Dictionary of Economics*, J. Eatwell, M. Milgate, and P. Newman, eds. (London: Macmillan, 1987), vol. 4, p. 521.

and his pupils.⁸ Spann claimed that all parts of the economy like households and firms could only be understood as elements of an organic whole. This contrasted sharply with the approach of the Austrian economists who sought to explain economic phenomena as resulting from individual action and from the social interaction of individuals (the principle of methodological individualism).

Single-handedly Strigl made an effective case for economic theory and methodological individualism in this intellectually hostile environment. His early death November 11, 1942 prevented him from making the post-World War II University of Vienna safe for the Austrian School. In an obituary for Strigl, F.A. Hayek mourned: "with his death disappears the figure on whom one's hope for a preservation of the tradition of Vienna as a centre of economic teaching and a future revival of the 'Austrian School' had largely rested."⁹

III

Strigl's *Capital and Production* is squarely rooted within the tradition of the Austrian School, that is, within the approach to economic analysis initiated by Carl Menger's work on economic principles.

Ever since the first publication of *Grundsätze der Volkswirtschaftslehre* in 1871, Mengerian economic analysis had inspired an increasing number of young economists in Austria and Germany. As a result, in the period from 1871 to 1940, each new generation of German-language Austrian economists was larger than the previous one.[10]

The second generation, active from the 1880s to the 1910s, comprised Menger's most brilliant followers Eugen von Böhm-Bawerk and Friedrich von Wieser, and a few lesser economists

---

[8]See for example Othmar Spann's *magnum opus*, *Der wahre Staat* (The True State) (Leipzig: Quelle and Meyer, 1921).

[9]Hayek, "Richard von Strigl," p. 285.

[10]On the impact of Menger's work on other countries, in particular on the United Kingdom and the United States of America, see Joseph T. Salerno's important work, "The Place of Mises's *Human Action* in the Development of Modern Economic Thought," *Quarterly Journal of Austrian Economics* 2, no. 1 (1999): 35–65.

such as Emil Sax. He also influenced Knut Wicksell, who at that time wrote and published in German.

By the early 1900s, the third generation—Strigl's generation—came into its own: Ludwig von Mises, Joseph Schumpeter, Hans Mayer, Karl Schlesinger, Franz Weiss, Leo Schönfeld-Illy, Franz Čuhel, Robert Liefmann, and others.

Then, in the 1920s, a fourth generation of Austrian economists arose which included F.A. Hayek, Fritz Machlup, Gottfried Haberler, Oskar Morgenstern, Ewald Schams, Paul Rosenstein-Rodan, Wilhelm Röpke, Walter Eucken, Friedrich Lutz, Ludwig Lachmann, Alexander Mahr, Karel Englis, and others. Some of these economists would become very famous after World War II, when they continued their career in the United States of America. Hayek, who received the 1974 Nobel Prize in economics, had a very strong impact on Austrian economists of the 1970s and 1980s.

Although Carl Menger influenced all these generations considerably, it is not surprising that individual contributions differed from one another in more or less important respects. Here two factors come into play.

On the one hand, other traditions than the one established by Menger often had a crucial impact on these economists. For example, Léon Walras influenced Wicksell's, Schumpeter's, and Schlesinger's work to such a degree that it would in fact be more appropriate to classify these men as Walrasian rather than Austrian economists. And Walter Eucken, Ludwig Lachmann, and other theoretically-minded economists from Germany labored under the legacy of the Historical School.

On the other hand, Menger's work was itself open to different interpretations, or at any rate inspired its readers in different ways, and his followers did not always share the same emphasis in the elaboration of his approach. Thus, for example, Wieser stressed what he perceived to be the psychological foundations of value theory whereas Böhm-Bawerk tended to emphasize the role of objective factors in the determination of value, such as quantities of goods and physical productivity. In Mises's eyes, human choice was the cornerstone of economic analysis. By contrast, the early Hayek and many other students of Mises's were particularly interested in the equilibrium relationships between market prices and the structure of production; and the later Hayek saw the acquisition and use of knowledge as the central problem of economic theory.[11]

Strigl was primarily interested in the scientific foundation of policy proposals, an interest that he shared with Ludwig von Mises. This concern for practical questions incited him to take particular care of methodological problems, and he was very effective in integrating methodological studies into his research. All in all, Böhm-Bawerk had the most lasting impact on Strigl, but as the reader of this volume will find, the ideas of Walras, Wieser, Schumpeter, and Mises also found their way into his writings.

IV

Richard von Strigl is the author of pioneering studies on economic theory, applied economics, capital theory, and the relationship between theoretical and historical research.

He published four books. Two of them deal with economic theory applied to specific areas: *Kapital und Produktion* and *Angewandte Lohntheorie* (Applied Wage Theory, 1926). In the latter work he showed himself an unabashed Böhm-Bawerkian, arguing that labor unions cannot increase the wages of all members of the working classes. His last book is an introduction to economic principles that F.A. Hayek called "probably the best modern introduction to economic theory available in German" at the

---

[11]It is therefore in many respects misleading to speak of "the" Austrian School of economics while in fact there are distinct and competing lines of the Austrian tradition. Two of these lines dominate the contemporary scene: on the one hand, the Menger–Böhm-Bawerk–Mises–Rothbard line and, on the other hand, the Menger–Wieser–Hayek–Kirzner line. See Murray N. Rothbard, "The Present State of Austrian Economics," *Journal des Economistes et des Etudes Humaines* 6, no. 1 (1995): 43–89; and Joseph T. Salerno, "Mises and Hayek Dehomogenized," *Review of Austrian Economics* 6, no. 2 (1993): 113–48, and "The Place of Mises's *Human Action* in the Development of Modern Economic Thought." Hans-Hermann Hoppe, "Einführung: Ludwig von Mises und der Liberalismus," in Ludwig von Mises, *Liberalismus* (Sankt Augustin: Academia Verlag, 1993) makes a compelling case that the Menger–Böhm-Bawerk–Mises–Rothbard line best reflects the essence of the Austrian tradition.

time.[12] Here he discusses the problems that would occupy the energies of the next two generations of neoclassical economists: the shape of the cost curve from which he hoped to derive a long-run supply curve, and pricing in different market structures, in particular competitive and monopoly prices.

Of particular interest is his first book, *Ökonomische Kategorien und die Organisation der Wirtschaft* (1923) which gained him at once a wide reputation and influenced many economists, in particular the younger ones who represent the fourth generation of Austrian economists.[13]

The book deals with methodological problems of economics and with the relationship between theoretical and historical research in the social sciences. Its title can most appropriately be translated as "fundamental economic concepts and the data of the economy." According to Strigl, economic science deals exclusively with states of affairs characterized by scarcity. All the relevant aspects of such states of affairs can be described with just four fundamental economic concepts: (1) economic subject, (2) ownership, (3) possible uses of a good, and (4) value scales. These concepts have the nature of general "forms" with the help of which one can classify or "capture" manifold "relative-historical contents." This classification of concrete reality by means of economic concepts is the task of descriptive economics, one of two branches of economic science.

The four fundamental concepts are also important because of certain necessary relationships that exist between these concepts—and thus, indirectly, between the relative-historical contents that correspond to the concepts in any concrete situation. Describing these relationships is the subject matter of theoretical economics, the other branch of economic science.

Because the fundamental concepts are formal, the relationships between them exist independently of their concrete content

---

[12]Hayek, "Richard von Strigl," p. 285. The title of Strigl's last book is *Einführung in die Grundlagen der Nationalökonomie* (Vienna: Manz, 1937).

[13]See Hayek, "Richard von Strigl," p. 285. See also the 1923 book review by Gottfried Haberler, "Economics as an Exact Science," in *Austrian Economics*, Israel M. Kirzner, ed. (London: William Pickering, 1994), vol. 2.

in any given historical situation. Thus, Strigl can concede to the economist of the Historical School that history is in constant flux and transformation as it shifts from one unique period to another. Yet this does not alter the fact that at all times and places there are (1) economic subjects who (2) own certain goods that (3) can be used in some ways, but not in others, and that (4) the way in which a good is used is chosen according to the individual's value scale. And since this is so, the laws described by economic theory exist always and everywhere, and economic theory thus contains universally valid propositions.

Hence, Strigl's fundamental economic concepts perform two important tasks. On the one hand, they serve to classify all relevant historical facts. They thereby "capture" empirical reality and link economic theory to the real world. On the other hand, they are themselves building blocks of economic theory, which in fact is nothing but a description of the relationships that exist between them. This approach to clarifying the link between theoretical and historical research has had a considerable influence in Austrian and German economics. The most important follower of Strigl was the great Freiburg economist Walter Eucken whose work can be considered as an elaboration of Striglian economics.[14]

Unfortunately, Strigl's works fell into almost complete oblivion. To a strong degree, this was the fate of the entire Austrian School in the Germanic countries. Their bastion had always been Vienna and it was from this center that their ideas spread to the rest of Austria and to Germany, Holland, Scandinavia, all of Eastern Europe, and the northern cantons of Switzerland. Yet beginning with the early 1930s, Vienna's Austrian-School culture died by exodus. Mises left for Switzerland where he found a prestigious position that would allow him to write his *magnum opus*. Hayek, Machlup, and Haberler departed for the United Kingdom or the United States, where they could obtain academic positions foreclosed to them back home. And after the 1938 *Anschluß*, many others left because Nazi Austria made life unbearable for Jews like Morgenstern and for all non-Jews who could not find or accept any *modus vivendi* with the National Socialist German Workers' Party.

---

[14]See Walter Eucken, *Kapitaltheoretische Untersuchungen* (Jena: Fischer, 1934), and *Grundlagen der Nationalökonomie*, 9th ed. (Berlin: Springer, [1939] 1989).

Although Strigl had remained as the last member of this group at the original home of the School, for him too life and work had become unbearable. His health was gravely affected and he was disgusted by the opportunistic behavior of many of his countrymen. Joseph Steindl wrote at the time:

> Since the invasion of Austria he has been silent; we have not heard of any further publication of his. This is not surprising to those who knew him, and it is probably not only due to an illness which befell him in 1939. The spectacle of the conversion overnight of so many to a new creed was not congenial to him who had so conspicuously lacked the talents of a careerist in all his professional life.[15]

With Strigl's death the Austrian School of economics ceased to exist as an independent force in post-World War II Austria and Germany. It became a closed chapter in the intellectual history of these countries and continued to thrive only in the United States, where Strigl's ideas are now finally beginning to receive the attention they deserve.

V

Capital and Production is an outstanding contribution to economic science and a splendid manifestation of the pedagogical talents of its author. Strigl proceeds in a step-by-step manner to give an account of the workings of the macroeconomy. This account is remarkable in two ways.

First, his argument makes much scarcer use of aggregates than John Maynard Keynes's *General Theory* which, published two years after *Capital and Production*, unfortunately set the standard for macroeconomic reasoning until our own times. But Strigl and Keynes differ not only in regard to the scope they attribute to the use of aggregates, but also in respect to the very use they

---

[15]Steindl as quoted in Hayek, "Richard von Strigl," p. 285. The outstanding example of a careerist was Hans Mayer who had found a *modus vivendi* with the Nazis, just as he would later make an arrangement with the Socialist Party of Austria, which would rule the country after World War II. It is therefore probably not only for doctrinal reasons that Hayek had called Strigl the "last" Austrian economist in Vienna, omitting Mayer.

make of them. Keynes and the mainstream of macroeconomists seek to uncover constant relationships between the aggregates themselves; for example, they look for constant relationships between the supply of money on the one hand, and the price-level, employment, and output on the other hand. By contrast, Austrian economists like Strigl are not interested in the relationships between aggregates unless they can trace them back to human decisionmaking and to the individual (or marginal) objects that human beings deal with in their actions. For Strigl, then, macroeconomics primarily consists in tracing the connections that exist between all individual prices and quantities "until a picture emerges in which each phenomenon is co-determined by every other, and in which the law-governed nature of the whole follows from the determining forces of each part" (p. 39).[16]

Second, Strigl builds his theory of the macroeconomy on an original account of the part played by different forms of capital. In particular, he stresses the fundamental role that consumer goods, or means of subsistence, play in connection with the fact that production takes time. When consumer goods are used to sustain laborers engaged in time-consuming roundabout production processes, they are used as "free capital" (p. 27). Since without sustenance for laborers no such roundabout production processes can be started at all, consumer-goods-used-as-capital are the most fundamental or "originary form" (p. 62) of capital.

This fundamental insight, that productively-used consumer goods are originary capital, had already been expressed in

---

[16]Low-aggregation analysis is a hallmark of Austrian capital theory. Yet Strigl surpasses in this respect most other Austrian capital theories. Knut Wicksell, *Über Kapital: Wert und Rente* (Jena: Fischer, 1893), *Geldzins und Güterpreise* (Jena: Fischer, 1898), and *Lectures on Political Economy* (London: Macmillan, 1934); Irving Fisher, *The Nature of Capital and Income* (New York: Kelley, [1906] 1965); F.A. Hayek, *Geldtheorie und Konjunkturtheorie*; Mark Skousen, *The Structure of Production* (New York: New York University Press, 1990); and even Murray N. Rothbard, *Man, Economy, and State*, 3rd ed. (Auburn, Ala.: Mises Institute, [1962] 1993), take recourse to higher degrees of aggregation than does Strigl (but to far lower degrees than the economic mainstream). Capital theories that strictly and entirely avoid reference to aggregates are in Ludwig von Mises, *Human Action*, Scholar's Edition (Auburn, Ala.: Mises Institute, 1998), chap. 28, Ludwig Lachmann, *Capital and its Structure*, 2nd ed. (Kansas City: Sheed, Andrews and McMeel, 1956), and Israel M. Kirzner, *An Essay on Capital* (New York: Kelley, 1966).

Jevons's wage-fund theory of capital, and it is still common stock in Austrian economics.[17] However, no one has surpassed Strigl in systematically analyzing the implications thereof, and in integrating these findings into a theory of the macroeconomy. His legacy to present-day capital theorists rests to a great extent mainly on this contribution.[18]

One important implication of this insight is that it is unwarranted to conceive of capital from a purely technological point of view. Machines, buildings, etc.—that is, those capital goods most readily identified with the notion of capital—are themselves products of previous production processes which, ultimately, make use of labor, land, and "productively-used" consumer goods. Moreover, capital goods can only be used if corresponding quantities of consumer goods are fed into the production process to sustain the laborers who work with these capital goods. Using capital goods in production processes and supporting these processes with consumer goods are nothing but two aspects of "one and the same process" (p. 24). In short, the quantities and qualities of capital goods in use at any time depend ultimately on what people choose to do with the consumer goods they control. A man can choose to use all his consumer goods in "pure consumption" or to use a part of them (his "savings") in "productive consumption"; that is, he can use this part to sustain himself or others while being engaged in a productive venture. Depending on such choices, consumer goods become either pure consumer goods or originary capital. Hence, whether one and the same

---

[17]See William Stanley Jevons, *Theory of Political Economy*, 5th ed. (New York: Kelley, [1871] 1956), pp. 223f.; Eugen von Böhm-Bawerk, *Positive Theorie des Kapitals*, 4th ed. (Jena: Fischer, 1921), p. 139; Mises, *Human Action*, pp. 488, 501; and Rothbard, *Man, Economy, and State*, p. 46.

[18]Also, Strigl anticipated the main tenets of George Reisman's net-consumption/net-investment theory of interest and profit (see Reisman's *Capitalism* [Ottawa, Ill.: Jameson Books, 1996], pp. 719ff.). Strigl insisted that (a) the rate of interest is codetermined by savings (the wage fund), marginal productivity, and the size of the "rations" (see pp. 68, 71) and that (b) the volume of interest payments and entrepreneurial profits corresponds exactly to the extent of pure consumption by entrepreneurs and capitalists. See pp. 56ff., 99, and 103.

physical object is capital depends ultimately on the choices of the market participants; capital formation has a subjective basis.[19]

Strigl then sets out to give a capital-based explanation of the business cycle by discussing the impact of the creation of "new money" on the real economy.[20] If the new money reaches the market in the form of a "credit expansion," that is, if it first reaches the credit market, then it will depress the interest rate below its equilibrium level. As a result, two shifts will occur in the structure of production: "First, when consumer-goods production is expanded, capital will be consumed; and second, when roundabout production is expanded there will be an increasing immobilisation of capital investments" (p. 131). The result is an overall impoverishment of society. This is, *in nuce,* Strigl's explanation of what caused the Great Depression.

The two appendices to *Capital and Production* merit particular attention. In the first one, Strigl deals with methodological problems and political implications of business cycle theory. The second, on the concept of capital, is a splendid general conclusion to the whole book. Here Strigl drives home his main point: that without proper attention to the role of the subsistence fund, capital theory goes astray. It was "all too concerned with outwardly visible occurrences: the supply of durable capital goods and the far-reaching synchronization of production" (p. 161). The result was the "nonsensical doctrine of a surplus of capital" (p. 162), that is, the contradiction of Say's Law, and the idea that synchronization makes time irrelevant (p. 163).

---

[19]This subjectivist nature of capital—the fact that capital is tied up with individual plans and choices—was later stressed by Mises, *Human Action*, pp. 488, 492; Lachmann, *Capital and its Structure*; and Kirzner, *An Essay on Capital*.

[20]This integration of capital theory and the theory of money into a business cycle theory was first outlined in Ludwig von Mises, *Theorie des Geldes und der Umlaufsmittel* (Munich and Leipzig: Duncker and Humblot, 1912), translated as *Theory of Money and Credit* (Indianapolis, Ind.: Liberty Fund, 1980). It became the hallmark of Austrian works on business cycle theory as manifested, for example, in the works by Hayek, Rothbard, and Skousen.

VI

Capital and Production has all the features of a classic of economic science: it is clear, profound, and systematic. Still it might be useful to comment on some aspects of Strigl's analysis that otherwise might escape attention. In particular, the following observations are meant as a guide for those readers who are not yet fully acquainted with the whole spectrum of Austrian works on capital-based macroeconomics.

Strigl's method of analysis is to focus on the static economy and on problems of reproduction of capital (see, for example, pp. 17, 38, 88f.). This was the methodological fashion of the day and Strigl shows himself a true master of the art of seamlessly integrating methodological and applied work. Today, equilibrium analysis is not very popular among many Austrian economists since it distracts attention away from what these modern scholars consider to be most important: uncertainty and institutions created to handle uncertainty. Yet even apart from questions of emphasis one may notice that Strigl's method has substantial repercussions for his analysis. For example, his emphasis on the reproduction of capital runs the risk of ignoring the fact that capital goods permit a lengthening of roundabout production by virtue of their mere existence (see Mises, *Human Action,* Scholar's Edition [Auburn, Ala.: Mises Institute, 1998], pp. 492, 495), even if they cannot be profitably reproduced.

Furthermore, so far as the general procedure of the analysis is concerned, Strigl does in fact not heed his announced intention (p. xxx) to first analyze a barter economy and only then turn to dissect the impact of the "veil of money." Rather, his discussion of the law of cost, crucial for his argument in chapter two, refers to money prices.[21] He correctly states: "Each factor of production whose marginal product can obtain a price larger than the price

---

[21]Let us observe in this context that Strigl lacks a clear distinction between value and physical productivity in his discussion of the law of diminishing marginal productivity and of the law of costs. He sets out (on pp. 48ff.) to discuss marginal productivity exclusively in physical terms. But when it comes to stating the law of costs, he switches to value terms; for now he compares prices paid for marginal physical products with prices paid for factors of production (see pp. 51f.). However, we can exculpate Strigl since the first satisfying account of the relationship between marginal physical productivity and marginal value

of this factor will be employed up to the point at which these two prices are equal." It follows that the two prices must be money prices since otherwise it would be impossible to tell whether they are equal or not. It is therefore best to read the second chapter, not as an account of the connectivity of prices in a barter economy, but as a description of the connectivity of money prices under the impact of nonmonetary factors. These are, for example, the supply of factors of production, the law of return, and interest.

It also has to be observed that Strigl completely neglects the political factors determining economic growth and the formation of the economy's structure of production. Apparently in the 1930s only Mises was courageous enough to point out that political organizations, like labor unions, were responsible for the unnecessary aggravation of the economic crisis of 1929. Strigl's account of the Great Depression, and Striglian interpretations of similar situations, as pertinent as they might be on behalf of the relationships between money, prices, and production, thus need to be complemented by an analysis of such political factors.[22]

Speaking now more narrowly about capital-based macroeconomics, we notice that Strigl does not offer a complete disaggregation of "capital." He distinguishes between free capital, intermediary products, and fixed capital. This is progress in comparison to the theoretical treatment of capital by most of his predecessors. And the three concepts are located on a much lower level of aggregation than "aggregate demand and supply" etc., which are still fashionable in modern economics. However, the fact remains that all these aggregates are aggregates and thus deal with the very heterogeneous goods that we find in reality as homogeneous blobs. As Mises would observe some years after *Capital and Production* appeared, there is no such thing as a class of free capital. There are only concrete and specific goods. Each is well suited only for the satisfaction of a very limited set of needs,

---

productivity (that is, marginal money-price productivity) was published almost thirty years later by Rothbard in *Man, Economy, and State*. Rothbard also emphasizes that factors of production earn the *discounted* value of their marginal product rather than, as Strigl (p. 72) asserts, the entire marginal product.

[22]See for example the studies by Murray N. Rothbard, *America's Great Depression*, 5th ed. (Auburn, Ala.: Mises Institute, 2000) and Richard Vedder and Lowell Gallaway, *Out of Work*, 2nd ed. (New York: New York University Press, 1997).

less suited to meet various other goals, and completely incapable of satisfying still other requirements. Presumably Strigl would have agreed; disaggregation of his three forms of capital would have been very much in the spirit of his general method: starting from a general, somewhat unrealistic model, and then step by step relaxing the unrealistic assumptions.

So far we have been concerned with relatively minor aspects of Strigl's analysis. Now we turn to some elements of his argument that have great practical relevance.

Strigl correctly notes that monetary calculation can enable market participants to gauge the quantity of the capital they own. However, in distinct contrast to Menger and Mises, who emphasize that a homogeneous and quantifiable capital exists only in the form of such aggregated money prices and has no counterpart in the physical world of heterogeneous goods,[23] Strigl insists that money can "represent" or "correspond to" capital. In short, Menger and Mises see homogeneous units of capital as *ontologically* bound up with money prices and calculation, whereas Strigl perceives this link as merely *nominal*. For him, there are homogeneous units of "capital" out there in the physical world. He believes that the system of money prices is nothing but a veil layered over a barter economy (see pp. 20, 91, 98, 100, 142); and so is the capital sum that results from monetary calculation just a veil overlaying a sum of physical capital.

If the calculated money capital adequately represents the quantities of physical capital, then money is neutral and the monetary economy is in equilibrium: that is, it operates just as a barter economy. By contrast, if money fails even slightly in its representation job then problems occur which manifest themselves in business cycles.

In Strigl's view, the representation of physical capital is rendered inaccurate by *all* money-induced price changes because he tacitly postulates *static expectations* on the side of all market participants. Thus, when banks create uncovered money titles and pump them into the credit market, then for Strigl "it is

---

[23]See Carl Menger, "Zur Theorie des Kapitals," *Gesammelte Werke*, 2nd ed. (Tübingen: Mohr, [1888] 1970), vol. 3; and Mises, *Human Action*, chaps. 11–13, 26.

clear" (p. 116) that this additional credit can *only* be accommodated at an interest rate lower than the equilibrium interest rate. The market participants do not take into account that the new money titles will bring about a price increase; rather, they assume that all prices will remain at the present level. Therefore, creditors do not ask for higher (equilibrium) interest rates and debtors do not bid them. More investment projects appear profitable than can be sustained with the available quantities of capital goods since money prices and interest no longer adequately represent the real supply of capital; an artificial "boom" is created which is doomed to break down in a crisis.

Accounting for the fact that expectations are not static but free leads to a different picture. The monetary calculus of market entrepreneurs essentially depends on the selling prices that these entrepreneurs expect to realize in an uncertain future. Only if they underestimate the impact of credit expansion on these prices will credit expansion depress the rate of interest below its equilibrium level. Only then will more investment projects appear profitable than can be sustained with the available quantities of capital goods; and only then will an artificial "boom" be created which is doomed to burst in a crisis.[24]

The static-expectations theory of money's impact on the structure of production is also the basis for Strigl's analysis of money hoarding.[25] From his perspective, increasing and decreasing money hoards both disrupt the representation of physical capital through money capital. Decreasing money hoards entail

---

[24]The clarification of the role of expectations in Austrian business cycle theory starts with Ludwig von Mises, *Nationalökonomie* (Geneva: Editions Union, 1940), p. 696, and the exchange between Ludwig Lachmann, "The Role of Expectations in Economics as a Social Science," *Economica* 10, no. 37 (1943): 12–23; and Ludwig von Mises, "'Elastic Expectations' and the Austrian Theory of the Business Cycle," *Economica* 10, no. 39 (1943): 251–52.

[25]We leave aside the problem that *all* sums of money are "hoarded." Any given unit of money can therefore not be hoarded more than it is already hoarded, and such fictional increased hoarding cannot be the cause of price changes. What is really at stake is that people choose to delay expenditures or to offer lower money prices in exchange for the goods and services they desire or offer more of their goods and services in exchange for the sums of money they desire. Yet such behavior does not *cause* prices to decrease; rather it is a *manifestation* of price decreases.

an economic upswing when the released money hoards first arrive on the credit markets and thus decrease interest rates below their equilibrium level. Increasing money hoards engender an economic downswing when the hoarded money is sucked out of the credit markets, thus pushing interest rates above their equilibrium level. Any change in money hoards is therefore bound to bring about booms and busts (see pp. 115ff., 140, 148f., 151).

In this analysis of the effects of hoarding Strigl advocated an argument that was prominent with the Wieserian line of Austrian economists. In their eyes, hoarding is inherently disruptive of economic equilibrium since it destroys the "correspondence" between money and the nonmonetary (capital) goods. This correspondence is only given insofar as the monetary economy mimics a barter economy through "complementary transactions."[26]

---

[26]See in particular Friedrich von Wieser, "Der Geldwert und seine Veränderungen," *Gesammelte Abhandlungen* (Tübingen: Mohr, 1928); F.A. Hayek, *Prices and Production*, pp. 118ff.; Fritz Machlup, *Börsenkredit, Industriekredit und Kapitalbildung*; and J.G. Koopmans, "Zum Problem des 'Neutralen' Geldes," in *Beiträge zur Geldtheorie*, F.A. Hayek, ed. (Vienna: Springer, 1933). Wieser was not the originator of these views, even though he was instrumental in spreading them among the younger Austrian economists. For a German predecessor of Wieser see Wilhelm Roscher, *Die Grundlagen der Nationalökonomie*, 6th ed. (Stuttgart, 1866), p. 446. Since we cannot go into much detail here, let us merely notice that the notion of a correspondence between money and other goods and the notion of compensatory transactions are fictitious stipulations; they have no basis in observed fact or other evidence. In particular, they both rely on the idea that economic calculation could be cast in terms other than in money prices. For only if there were such a *tertium comparationis* would it make sense to assert that a correspondence between money and other goods might or might not exist. However, since adding and subtracting money prices is the very essence of economic calculation (see Mises, *Human Action*, chaps. 11–13, and 26), this assertion is groundless. Moreover, the claim that money prices do not really correspond to the good bought, whereas correspondence always exists in barter transactions, implicitly denies that money is a good. Finally, as we have pointed out before, the success of market participants and, therefore, the equilibrium of the economy, exclusively depend on the correctness of their expectations about the future. These expectations do adapt to changes in conditions (like hoarding) and they can adapt instantaneously, and can even anticipate such changes in the future. It is thus unwarranted to claim that hoarding *inherently* entails a disruption of the equilibrium of the economy. See on this last point, for example, Mises, *Human Action*, p. 578; and Rothbard, *America's Great Depression*, part 1.

For example, suppose that in a barter economy one apple is exchanged against one pear. Here the apple supply is confronted by a corresponding demand in the form of the pear and, inversely, the pear supply is confronted by a corresponding demand in the form of the apple. With the introduction of money, this direct exchange is split up in two monetary exchanges: the apple is exchanged against, say, one ounce of copper and the copper coin is then exchanged against the pear. These two monetary exchanges are complementary transactions in the sense that, together, they bring about a result that had also obtained in the barter economy. Since both the apple and the pear are exchanged against the same sum of money, for the owner of the apple everything is as if he had exchanged the apple against the pear in a barter transaction. So far so good.

The twist in the argument comes from the assumption that monetary exchanges are nothing but a veil layered over an underlying barter economy. Money therefore does not count as a good, and there is no demand for and supply of money per se. Money traded in market exchanges merely represents other goods that it can buy. Only these other goods truly correspond to the goods against which money is exchanged. In our example, when the copper coin is traded for the apple, the coin is not desired as a good. It merely represents the pear. And it is the pear that truly "corresponds" to the apple in this exchange.

It follows that by looking at a single monetary transaction (apple against an ounce of copper) one cannot tell whether the apple supply has a corresponding demand. One has to wait until it comes to a complementary transaction. However, whereas in a barter economy demand and supply always and necessarily correspond to one another, such a correspondence may not exist in a monetary economy. Suppose for example that the seller of the apple does not proceed to exchange his ounce of copper against a pear, but instead hoards it. In this case, according to the Wieserian monetary economists, there exists a money-induced disequilibrium. As Hayek said:

> the identity of demand and supply, which must necessarily exist in the case of barter, ceases to exist as soon as money becomes the intermediary of the exchange transactions. [Problems will arise] when after the division of the barter

transaction into two separate transactions, one of these takes place without the other complementary transaction. In this sense demand without corresponding supply, and supply without a corresponding demand, evidently seem to occur in the first instance when money is spent out of hoards (i.e., when cash balances are reduced), when money received is not immediately spent, when additional money comes on the market, or when money is destroyed.[27]

This is the basis for Hayek's assertion that "any change in the velocity of circulation would have to be compensated by a reciprocal change in the amount of money in circulation if money is to remain neutral towards prices."[28]

Strigl pushes this theory to its ultimate conclusion when he makes the case for the existence of business cycles on the free market (see pp. 147ff.). During the bust phase of the business cycle money hoards are built up, and at the end of this phase these hoards are dissolved and return into circulation, thereby upsetting the representation of physical capital in monetary calculation. A new boom ensues, which is however doomed to end up in another bust, and so the free market goes on, oscillating mechanically between upswings and downswings.

These views about the significance of money hoarding explain why Strigl did not share Ludwig von Mises's categorical rejection of "additional credit," that is, credit created by banks in the form of money titles that are not backed by money actually saved.[29] Strigl points out that additional credit *can* involve a "credit expansion" which pushes interest rates below their equilibrium level and thus brings about a boom-bust cycle (pp. 114ff.). However, he thinks that additional credit *can also* have the

---

[27]Hayek, *Prices and Production*, p. 130.

[28]Ibid., p. 124.

[29]Mises, *Theorie des Geldes und der Umlaufsmittel*, called this type of credit "Zirkulationskredit" (circulation credit or fiduciary credit) and rejected it in this and in all of his later writings, even though it was only in the 1940s that he thoroughly explained why there could be no such thing as a "compensatory credit." See Joseph T. Salerno, "Mises and Hayek Dehomogenized," *Review of Austrian Economics* 6, no. 2 (1993): 113–48 on this development of Mises's monetary thought.

healthy and even necessary function of compensating for those changes in monetary circulation that stem from money hoarding (pp. 117f.). These "compensatory credits" make the volume of credits "elastic" and thus help assure monetary equilibrium.[30]

One implication of these views on money and credit is that there is a scope for anticyclical economic policy, which would include creating compensatory credit. Strigl affirms this implication. However, he hastens to point out that such a policy is not much more than a mere theoretical possibility since the obstacles to the creation of compensatory credit are formidable. In particular, he mentions the knowledge problem of the monetary authorities (see pp. 152ff.). Thus, although he disagrees with Mises and later writers who denied the very possibility of anticyclical policy, Strigl is quite close to these thinkers when it comes to the political applications of his theory.

VII

The purpose of the foregoing comments was to highlight some rather subtle aspects of Strigl's analysis of capital, prices, and production. It goes without saying that his rich analysis cannot be exhaustively presented in our introduction. Students of capital-based macroeconomics will have to become thoroughly acquainted with it on their own. The rewards will be great, though, as *Capital and Production* is a timeless classic of economic literature.

Thanks are due to those who made the English translation even more beautiful and useful than the German original: to Professor and Mrs. Hoppe for the translation, to Mr. Jeffrey Tucker and Professor Larry Sechrest for careful revisions of the whole

---

[30]Very similar views are still maintained today, for example, in the works of George Selgin, *The Theory of Free Banking* (Totowa, N.J.: Rowman and Littlefield, 1988); and Leland B. Yeager, *The Fluttering Veil* (Indianapolis, Ind.: Liberty Fund, 1997). Selgin is in fact the present-day intellectual heir to the Wieserian approach to the analysis of money and banking. His main thesis is that banking systems without a central bank are best suited to adjust the supply of money to the demand thereof. For criticisms of this thesis see J.G. Hülsmann, "Banks Cannot Create Money," *Independent Review* 5, no. 1 (2000): 101–10 and the literature quoted there.

manuscript, to Mr. Richard Perry who compiled the index, and especially to the donors of the Mises Institute who made the rediscovery of Strigl possible.

Jörg Guido Hülsmann*
Auburn, Alabama, August 2000

---

*Jörg Guido Hülsmann is a Senior Fellow of the Ludwig von Mises Institute.

Foreword

The following investigation of the role of capital in production is based on the law of the higher productivity of roundabout methods of production and on the closely related theory of the wage fund. It thus grows out of propositions which have long been known to economic theory, and it is not our task to add much new to the various theorems that can be found in the realm of the theory of capital. First and foremost, I sought to elaborate, starting from a relatively broad general foundation, the abovementioned ideas, thus integrating the theory of capital into a theory of the macro-economy. Further, in contrast to a point of view which seems to me to adhere to a rather rigid conception of capital, I was especially interested in explaining the idea that capital is something that is employed in a permanent process of investment and release. The method that is applied is that of strict economic theory. For this reason, in addition to some knowledge of the basics of economics, understanding my arguments presupposes above all the ability and willingness to think abstractly. I must emphasize this here because perhaps more than is commonly done, I repeatedly build on simplified assumptions whose usefulness can be proved only in retrospect once the knowledge of the most general relationships can be used to explain more complex facts. That this method of economic theory also presupposes the ability and willingness to refrain from making value judgments and to inquire solely about relationships should be obvious. Regarding the topic treated here, let it be said explicitly that a study of the function of capital in the process of production has nothing to do with defending any particular organizational form of an economy. Although today—perhaps not solely out of resentment—the present economic order is often accused of letting the profit interest of capital work to the detriment of the economy, from the standpoint developed in the following study one can say that, in the process of an exchange economy, capital can only be conceived of as a subservient means in a process of the production of consumer goods. If the just-mentioned accusation has any justification, it can only be that through some institutional arrangements which are not an essential part of an exchange economy, an exemptory status has been granted to some—but not all—capital. Only then can it happen that this capital makes claims of the sort that goals which could otherwise be attained in the economy should be subordinate to its own interests. This has nothing to do with the subject of my study, yet I could not avoid occasionally making very brief remarks on relationships of this sort, though, without thereby discussing the vast, underlying problem exhaustively.

As far as presentation is concerned, it was necessary to first analyze a barter setting before analyzing an economy that uses money and credit. In so doing, I could not avoid occasionally reaching beyond the narrow realm of an analysis of the process of production. This is especially true of the first part of the second chapter. Here I had to follow the entire path, from the analysis of the supply of means of production up to the derivation of the law of marginal productivity, because in so doing I was searching for the formulation of a general principle which could also be applied to the theory of capital. I believe that only at this point has brevity of presentation been subordinated to the need for a comprehensive system built on a solid foundation. Apart from this, let it be said that my investigation only considers *one* large problem area; it should be accused neither of ignoring other problems nor of leaving out special questions which arise on lower levels of abstraction.

Richard von Strigl
Vienna, March 1934

CAPITALIST PRODUCTION

1. Factors of Production

Since nature has not provided man with all that he needs for his livelihood and to satisfy his further-reaching needs, he must constantly strive to produce consumer goods. The process of production was accurately described by Eugen von Böhm-Bawerk when he spoke of a *combination* of human labor and the gifts of nature. Human nature and those fruits of nature which are not so abundant that they suffice for all needs (and which are thus scarce) thereby become objects of "economizing"; that is, these factors of production will be used in such a way that the greatest possible return for some expenditure will be sought, and those expenditures will be avoided which cannot be justified in view of their expected results. In economic history, production has without a doubt grown extraordinarily, in spite of the fact that nature has provided the economy with only a limited supply of her best: her best soil, her best raw materials. Various circumstances have contributed to this increase in production. Above all, steady growth in the knowledge of the laws of nature has made it possible that new technical methods of production could always be found. Parallel to this was the progressive utilization of the advantages of combining the work of a number of people in various ways, especially in the form of division of labor, which successfully increased production by partitioning and simultaneously integrating productive operations. Finally, it is of utmost significance that man was able to draw on that element in the process of production that is identified with the term capital.

Labor and land (insofar as the best qualities are not available in superabundance) have been called the originary factors of production, and these have been contrasted with capital as a produced factor of production. However, if one accepts this formulation, one may not forget that when employing capital, one is never employing a new type of factor of production, but rather is using originary factors of production in a special way—since it can only have been produced out of originary factors of production. Whenever we speak of production capital, we must refer to the use of originary factors of production, the circumstances under which originary factors of production are used, and their effects. He who keeps this most obvious point in mind will easily avoid making many mistakes that derive from misguided speculation. We will see immediately that capital initially has nothing to do with money: "money capital" can only be an expression of relationships in a money economy.[1] Capital also cannot be something peculiar to a specific kind of social organization. Production "employs capital" or is "capitalist production" if it uses originary factors of production in a specific way, regardless of whether it is organized in a "capitalist way," which commonly means that private ownership of capital plays a specific social role. Finally, capital can be conceived of even less as a force of production that lies outside the reality of the world of goods, as an imaginary fund of productive achievements or something similar. To go astray here is most dangerous for economic theory.

The following discussion will first explain the essence of capital-employing production starting from well-known doctrines. We will only develop these doctrines insofar as they will later serve us as the foundation for our discussion of the phenomena of a market economy. For this reason, some of what would need to be explained in presenting a complete theory of capital will be absent here and will only be discussed later, and then only as regards its particular appearance within a market economy.

2. Roundabout Production

Human labor can be employed in production such that its direct goal is the finished product. An appropriate example,

---

[1]This formula does not rule out the possibility that changes in the structure of production can be affected from the side of money. More will be said on this later.

repeatedly cited since the times of Wilhelm Roscher, is of a nation of fishermen who directly employ their labor for the purpose of catching fish. This labor will reach a higher degree of productivity if the fishermen are able to produce a boat and other fishing tools. In this case, labor first must be expended in order to produce these "produced factors of production," but the reward for this expenditure will be a greater return. The essence of this process has been seen (Jevons and Böhm-Bawerk) in the combination of human labor and fruits of nature (natural resources) that are directed into a time-consuming roundabout method of production.

Here, the fishermen are faced with the task of increasing the product. Such an increase would be possible by employing more laborers: If the population increases, it can be expected that (given a sufficient amount of fish) an increase in the number of working hands will also lead to a larger harvest. However, in choosing a roundabout method of production we are concerned with another way of increasing the return while the number of laborers remains unchanged. Labor will now no longer be used directly for "momentary production" in order to achieve a finished product, but instead it will be redirected into a roundabout method of production. It will first be used to produce factors of production with whose help, and with the help of additional labor, the finished product will be attained. While this method of production will lead to an increase in returns as compared to the case of "momentary production," a longer period of time will elapse between the initial employment of labor and the final attainment of the finished product. Not only in modern times, but since the rise of man above the most primitive civilization, almost every act of production has been performed using a roundabout method of production; hardly anything that man eats or otherwise uses could have been attained without roundabout methods of production.

The general thesis would then read: An increase in the returns of production is not only possible by increasing the factors of production, but also by lengthening the roundabout methods of production, i.e., by using the same number of factors of production in such a way that more time elapses between their initial employment in production and the attainment of the finished product.

Metaphorically, this formula may be used: A sacrifice of time permits a greater output.

Regarding this thesis it should be noted that:

1. Not every lengthening of the roundabout method of production will necessarily lead to an increase in output. Rather, of all possible ways of lengthening the roundabout methods of production, an "intelligent choice" (Böhm-Bawerk) must be made in order to find those that will result in increased output.

2. Lengthening the roundabout method of production means that factors of production are not employed directly and without delay for the creation of a product, but instead that these factors of production are first rerouted for the creation of intermediary products out of which the final end product then results (usually with the help of additional factors of production). With the selection of additional roundabout methods of production, the length of time between the employment of the factors of production and the attainment of the finished product is increased. A lengthening of the roundabout method of production occurs every time the starting point for using factors of production is moved to an earlier point in time in the production process.

3. Increasing returns is to be understood as achieving a more advantageous ratio between the amount of factors of production expended and the amount of products produced. Thus, a greater amount of products will be achieved per factor of production as a result of lengthening the roundabout production method. We will only be able to measure this clearly if we begin by considering a single factor of production, for instance the expenditure of human labor of equal quality. Only then can the number of factors of production used be summed up and compared to the output. Where it is a question of using several different kinds of factors of production, we will later find a simple formula, which, in this case, will also permit the establishment of a relationship between expenditure and return.

4. Later we will have to prove that with repeated lengthening of the roundabout methods of production, the output always grows more slowly. Here this is only presented as a suggestion; we will need to prove this proposition before we draw conclusions from its application.

The law of greater productivity of roundabout methods of production can be validated without difficulty in economic reality. There can be no doubt that production constantly takes place in roundabout ways, and in always lengthened ways; for no one would have an interest in initiating time-consuming roundabout methods of production unless an increased return were the result.[2] From a purely economic standpoint, what one commonly calls improved production must almost always be understood as lengthening roundabout methods of production—except when it is exclusively attributable to progress of the division of labor or technological knowledge. For example, when a farmer produces grain—a production process whose length is determined by the natural ripening process of the plants—and uses chemicals as fertilizer, he thereby uses "previously done" labor to increase his harvest. He uses something in his production process which is the result of previously expended originary factors of production. Whenever a farmer uses machines in production, the roundabout method of production is lengthened in the same way because previously expended factors of production are thereby made available for current production. If an automobile is produced on a conveyor system (mass produced) rather than built in a unit-production mechanical garage, again machines will generally be used which are the product of previously expended factors of production that will only later yield a result. Why is all this done? Simply because as a result of lengthening the roundabout method of production, output increases.

And it can be seen clearly that the essence of this process of changing production does not lie in the use of more or different factors of production. It is true that other factors of production are used in the sense that the results of previous labor—fertilizer, machines, etc.—are something different from those factors of

---

[2]Cf. the discussion of the cooperation between factors of production on pp. 65ff. and 103ff.

production which were used alone at an earlier time. However, one should not limit oneself to a purely technological viewpoint. These new factors of production, too, are achievements of labor and natural gifts which have been used previously. If one thinks of these factors of production as the result of using originary factors of production, then the essence of this process lies in the fact that these originary factors of production were used at an earlier point in time. No one should confuse the use of machinery in production with an increased use of originary factors of production in the course of a roundabout method of production that is unchanged with respect to time.

Some choose to identify the "produced factors of production," which appear in the roundabout method of production, with the term capital. The formula of the greater productivity of roundabout methods of production, then, is simply expressed as follows: Employing capital (formerly expended originary factors of production) increases the output of production. We do not wish to run the risk of placing our explanations on unsteady ground by prematurely introducing the ambiguous and disputed concept of capital. For this reason we will avoid using this term. The essence of every process of production that uses capital can come into existence only because something had been produced with originary factors of production earlier which can now be used for further production. We will now occupy ourselves with the question of the possibility of an earlier use of factors of production in order to later attain a finished product. Thereby, it will be to our advantage to ignore everything that may be connected with any preconceived concept of capital. We will seek a definition of the concept of capital only after we have clarified the function of capital in roundabout methods of production.

3. The Length of Roundabout Production

Let us assume that in some country production must be completely rebuilt. The only factors of production available to the population besides laborers are those factors of production provided by nature. Now, if production is to be carried out by a roundabout method, let us assume of one year's duration, then it is self-evident that production can only begin if, in addition to these originary factors of production, a subsistence fund is available to the population which will secure their nourishment and any other needs for a period of one year. The population would in any case have an interest in stretching the roundabout method of production as long as possible, as every "cleverly chosen" lengthening of the roundabout method of production results in increased output. The extent to which the roundabout method of production can be lengthened is restricted, however, by the limited nature of the subsistence fund. The greater this fund, the longer is the roundabout factor of production that can be undertaken, and the greater the output will be.

It is clear that under these conditions the "correct" length of the roundabout method of production is determined by the size of the subsistence fund or the period of time for which this fund suffices. If a shorter roundabout method of production were begun with a subsistence fund that suffices for one year, then the output would be smaller than it could have been. However, if the roundabout method of production is too long, then it could not be completed without interruption. Let the possibilities that would arise be mentioned here. If a roundabout method of production of about two years' length is attempted, and if after one year the population realizes that half-finished products are being produced with which a greater output could be attained in an additional year, but there would be nothing left to live off of during this second year, then the roundabout method of production would have to be discontinued. The population would have to attempt to live "from hand to mouth" and get along with whatever could be produced daily in "momentary production."[3] Naturally, it will be less than it would have been if the roundabout method of the production in relation to the nature-given wealth of the land is too large; it will not even be possible to support the population, and some of them will starve. However, stopping a

---

[3]Even "momentary production" is a physical process which takes place in time. The roundabout method of production, however, lasts for an "economically relevant" period of time; that is, a time, as explained earlier, between the introduction of the originary factor of production and the achievement of the product that can only be bridged if a provision is possible through already finished means of subsistence.

too lengthy roundabout process of production altogether is not the only possibility available here. If the population realizes in time that the subsistence fund is running out, then—ignoring here the possibility of shortening the rations in which the subsistence fund is used up—it can also attempt to shorten the once-begun roundabout production in order to attain an earlier return. This return, however, will be smaller than that attainable with unhindered continuation of the roundabout method of production. But it will still be greater than that which can be attained through momentary production. This shortening of the roundabout method of production can be imagined such that part, perhaps about half, of the already begun production is continued, while the other part of production is stopped. The continued production is finished more quickly by means of an increased use of originary factors of production, in particular, of labor. We will have more to say about this process of shortening roundabout production later. Here we have only given a very general outline. It is clear that we still must answer the question of how a shortening of the roundabout method of production is *technically* possible, and hence whether and how it can happen that a roundabout method of production that is already in progress can be shortened.[4]

We must keep in mind that the size of the subsistence fund which supports the population for the duration of the roundabout method of production determines the length of the roundabout method of production. The problem of the roundabout method of production arises apparently from the fact that continuous support of the population is necessary, while the expenditure of originary factors of production, insofar as it occurs in

---

[4]The borderline between "momentary production" that brings the continuation of roundabout methods of production to a complete halt and merely shortening the roundabout method of production will have to be drawn sharply for a purely theoretical analysis. In practice, even the former case of the use of half-finished products will be possible in some way. For us, however, the sharp theoretical differentiation is of importance. Shortening the roundabout methods of production, it will be possible to maintain shortened roundabout methods of production under certain conditions, whereas the employment of the half-finished products in the process, which we here call momentary production, must, in a yet to be described sense, be considered capital consumption.

time-consuming roundabout methods of production, will only later provide a return in the form of means of subsistence.

Now it will be necessary to change our example somewhat and to conjure up a picture that more clearly reflects the situation of a real economy. We will keep the above in mind in order to have the problem of the length of roundabout methods of production permanently at our fingertips. If we wish to present the just mentioned feature of production graphically, we will represent the length of time for which production expenditure is successively fed into the roundabout production as a straight line. Production will be started at a point in time. After the completion of a time **t** (perhaps one year,[5] as in the previously mentioned example), production is finished. All originary factors of production have been expended during this time for products emerging out of a single roundabout production process. With these products, the economy has achieved a new subsistence fund which, after completion of time **t** and upon repeating the same roundabout method of production, will have been produced anew. It is not necessarily the case that after time **t** the acquired subsistence fund will suffice again for the same amount of time, i.e., that it is at least as large as was the initial fund. Yet, this will be explained later in connection with a discussion of the relationship between expenditures (costs) and revenue. Here we must pass by this question.

In the reality of modern production, the situation as compared to this simple case is different in many respects. But it will not be difficult to expand the just developed simple model by incorporating several further assumptions so that it takes on a form in which the appearance of today's production becomes completely clarified in its essence.

Now it was a very unrealistic assumption in our outline when we assumed that the entire production of a country would be started anew at one point in time and production would be carried out from beginning to end by making use of a given subsistence fund. In fact, we always see several production processes

---

[5]It would, however, be advantageous not to think thereby of the one-year duration of farm production. This is the case because even here the roundabout method of production can actually be longer—as a result of previously expended labor.

occurring simultaneously and in such a way that the individual production processes are finished at different times. We now would like to incorporate this fact of "synchronizing production" (John Bates Clark) into our model in a starkly stylized way. Hence, production does not occur in a single process, but rather it will be divided into several—as we here would still like to assume, equal—parts, such that within the time frame **t** (for example, one year) six independent production processes will be completed. Each production process—as we will again assume to simplify matters—produces the same kind of product in roundabout methods of production of equal lengths, and every production process will be repeated at its finish. We will represent this case as follows.

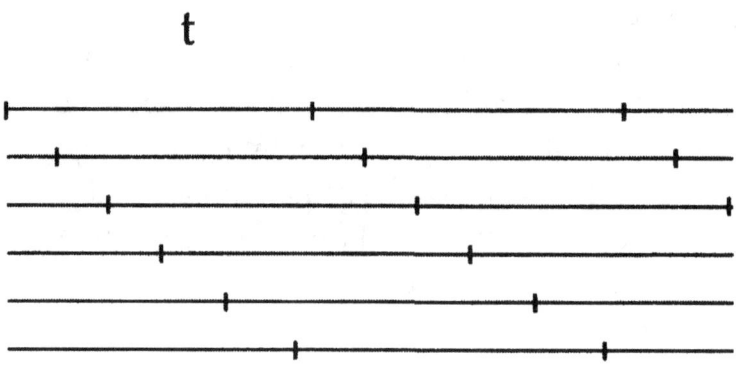

We are interested here in the role of the subsistence fund. It is immediately clear that at the completion of every production process, a subsistence fund of the size of one-sixth of that subsistence fund will be available which in the first case of a single uninterrupted production process was considered necessary. During the entire time **t**, the subsistence fund available to the population will be of the same size as in the first case. The reason, however, that at the completion of one of the six production processes the subsistence fund must not be at hand in its entire size is that in addition to the final subsistence fund, there exist five as yet incomplete subsistence funds at various stages of maturity. In carrying out production in a single process, we saw at the beginning a subsistence fund of a certain size which during the duration of the roundabout method of production successively declined until in the end it was completely exhausted. Simultaneously, a new subsistence fund grew. In the present case being analyzed, however, the subsistence fund available at the end of production has only one-sixth of the former's size. But this is compensated for by the fact that an unfinished equal-sized subsistence fund already exists at such a stage of maturity that it can replace the present funds as soon as this is exhausted.

Before we analyze even more realistic situations, we would like to point out something whose importance for roundabout methods of production we will only later understand. Here the formulation will appear as self-evident.

The six-fold partitioned process of production, in which one part is, so to speak, integrated with another, can of course only be carried out over time *if after completion of each of these parts the acquired subsistence fund is in fact used again to take up new production*, that is in "support" of this production.[6] Since here we are considering the process of production which involves roundabout methods of production without regard to a specific socioeconomic system, we must state this proposition in this form and only note that the way in which a subsistence fund is used further in production takes on very different appearances, depending on the socioeconomic order. If such production is carried out under the rule of an economic dictator in a centrally directed economy, he will assign this acquired subsistence fund to the residents of the country, but he will also see to it that they continue to work. If, on the other hand, in a market economy based on division of labor, production is directed by a plurality of independent entrepreneurs who acquire factors of production in exchange for their products, then production will only be continued if the attained consumption goods in turn serve to "purchase" factors of production. Regardless of the kind of socioeconomic order, if the once acquired subsistence fund is exhausted, the continued production would experience a disruption: It would show that after exhausting the subsistence fund, a further supply of means of

---

[6]We would like to use the previously mentioned expression "support" here as a *terminus technicus*. It will later be shown that a process is thereby described which in a monetary economy is labeled "financing."

sustenance is not available. Let this self-evident proposition be stated in a brief formula. Production can only be maintained if each attained subsistence fund is used to support another roundabout method of production. It is not, then, the fact that a subsistence fund exists which makes the continuation of production possible, but the way in which this subsistence fund is used: It must not be used in a "purely consumptive" way, but rather in the sense of "reproductive consumption," in the sense of consumption which simultaneously assures further production.

With this—later we will have to come back to it in a very different connection—we have pointed out two notions for characterizing the function of the subsistence fund in the framework of roundabout production processes. There must *first* be products which are appropriate for physically supporting the population, and second, these consumption goods must be used in such a way that, simultaneous to their expenditure, a later attainment of a new return of consumption goods is assured.

And now we can turn to further expanding our explanatory model. Only a few short comments need be mentioned because they do not significantly alter anything mentioned thus far. Essentially, nothing is changed in our explanation if we drop the assumption that each of the various integrated production processes results in the same consumption goods. In our graph (page 10), we can imagine a multitude of roundabout methods of production being placed at the points of the six integrated roundabout methods of production, with each producing a different product. Also, we can easily assume that the length of the roundabout method of production in the various production processes will be different too. After further extending a roundabout method of production in some production processes this may indeed be the case, depending on the extent of productivity. More will be said on this later. Nothing about the relationship between subsistence funds and roundabout methods of production changes if it is only assured that on the one hand, the subsistence fund which makes the roundabout method of production possible is continually maintained at a sufficient size and in an appropriate composition, and, on the other hand, that the roundabout methods of production are extended as far as the size of the subsistence fund permits. Finally, we will be able to include in our explanation the fact that production is so frequently partitioned in practice that in most production processes, products are completed in very brief periods of time; for many products, daily. Longer intervals between the production of any two contributions to the subsistence fund will occur primarily wherever production is tied to the rhythm of the seasons or where demand varies seasonally.

Let us once more return to a consideration of a simple model. Let us assume that, with an overall length of the roundabout method of production of one year, an equal part of the product is finished every week. The result would be that the subsistence fund available for the continuation of production is reduced to the size of the demands of one week. In addition to the subsistence fund, we always find unfinished products in the various stages of maturity. The supply of unfinished products is built up in such a way that in each following week a subsistence fund large enough for one week's needs will be finished. Each time, the finished available subsistence fund of the economy is reduced to a minimum. Yet, it is clear even in this case that the continuation of production is only possible if this subsistence fund is again used so that the various integrated production processes can be carried on continuously. The more elaborate the temporal partitioning of production into a number of synchronized production processes, the smaller the finished available subsistence funds will be. The always available subsistence fund will be reduced in importance even more as compared to the overall supply of goods in various stages of maturity. But note that nothing changes regarding the function of the subsistence fund. Maintaining roundabout production requires that a fund of consumer goods is regularly produced which is used to further support this production.

But now yet another decisive step must be taken. We have so far assumed that roundabout methods of production are always carried out in such a way that originary factors of production are employed and that labor is successively expended until the product is finished, at which time the same process begins anew, this is by no means unrealistic in the sense that such production would not be possible. But such production would be highly inefficient. To employ machines in a production process which ultimately would lead to the production of a consumer good, for example, one would have to start with the production of iron immediately. Only once the next roundabout method of production is at the same stage the iron production would have to begin anew. It is thus a great advantage to the integration (synchronization) of production processes that the production of raw materials used in these various production processes can proceed continuously. The individual roundabout method of production thus encompasses different firms, so to speak, which continuously make contributions to each of the roundabout production processes.

Now we have to take account of the fact that to a greater or lesser extent almost every firm uses produced factors of production which make contributions to a large number of production processes. Originally the individual roundabout method of production had been conceived of in such a way that originary factors of production were employed. With the expenditure of additional originary factors, the resulting "intermediate product" was transformed into the finished product; thus, the various intermediate products were only produced for the purpose of a *single* act of production. Now the situation has changed insofar as from now on "durable factors of production" will be produced. This kind of produced factor of production has been a much more frequent subject of treatments of the problems of production than the subsistence fund of which we have spoken so far. However, we will soon see that both must be considered simultaneously for an understanding of the phenomenon of roundabout production, and, in both cases, we are ultimately faced with one and the same problem.

4. Relatively Durable Factors of Production

The essence of the roundabout method of production can be seen clearly. Imagine that human labor employs raw materials which, with further labor and perhaps the help of other natural resources, in time turn into finished consumer goods. Once the finished product is attained, no other result of the expenditures of factors of production significant for further production remains. Throughout the various stages of the developing product, the maturing material changes into the finished consumer good and thus the process of production is completed.

This viewpoint is incomplete insofar as it ignores that, as a rule, production generates means that remain available for further production. Even in the most primitive production processes, tools are used which are relatively durable compared with the individual process of creating a finished product. In modern production, the use of such factors of production generally described as "machines" is of the greatest importance. It is necessary to emphasize again that the essence of roundabout production does not depend on the use of "produced factors of production" of this kind. Every production process which progresses past the stage of "hand to mouth" and takes on a "sacrifice of time," of "waiting" from the initial employment of originary factors of production until the product is attained, must, due to the fact that production serves the purpose of supplying human wants and can only be justified insofar as it serves this purpose, depend on the condition that it is integrated into a framework of continuously supplying people. Such a production process might be technically "correct" or even the best, but it will be economically inefficient or impossible if it is not structured in such a way that it adjusts to the scarcity of the various existing and maturing means of subsistence. If originary factors of production are used today that only later provide a return of consumer goods, and if nothing is available before the completion of these consumer goods for the necessary provisions, then the introduction of this production process must prove erroneous. In the process of employing originary factors of production in order to later achieve a finished product, the production of durable factors of production is only one special case. Here, too, nothing essentially happens other than that the originary factors of production available today are used for the purpose of attaining a future return. The peculiarity is only that in producing "machines," a relatively large number of originary factors of production are expended ("invested"), while the later incorporation of relatively few additional factors of production in addition to the achievements of the machines, can continuously yield a relatively large return over a longer period of time. And the greater the investment of originary factors of production in such durable factors of production, the more the relationship between the still-necessary expenditures and the revenue changes. If, however, the generally recognized advantage of this way of structuring the roundabout method of production is that a very significant increase in returns can be achieved relative to the expenditures of originary factors of production, then it is clear that nothing else is at hand here than the choice of particularly lengthy roundabout methods of production.[7]

We now must ask which general considerations are important for the integration of such production processes into the framework of a "correctly" structured production system. When we pointed out that, in general, a relatively large extension in the roundabout method of production is present here, it is clear that here, too, as for the previously mentioned structure of roundabout methods of production, the limitations of the subsistence fund available between the first expenditure of factors of production and the attainment of a finished product must be a decisive constraint for the length of the roundabout methods of production.

The production of a greater amount of durable factors of production requires a relatively large subsistence fund. It is only possible if a previously created (or continuously maturing) subsistence fund can support the population during the investment period. However, once the investment has been made, only a relatively brief period of production is necessary for the purpose of completing the now possible production processes. The once-made investment represents the economy's wealth and implies the possibility of attaining a large return with relatively few additional factors of production. Hence, this investment in durable factors of production appears as an independent factor of production. It is a means of increasing production which exists independent of the originary factors of production. A new, independent, third

---

[7]The "production time," i.e., the time needed for the processing of the individual parts of material into a finished product, will often be shorter with the increased use of durable factors of production. If one seeks a relationship to the length of the roundabout method of production here, then one can say that the length of the production process will generally be shorter, the longer the roundabout method of production is, i.e., the more durable factors of production are being used. We refer to the well-known example of Böhm-Bawerk regarding the sewing machine; in recent developments a shortening of the production time has been seen with remarkable frequency.

production factor is now created. Its creation was dependent on the fact that a subsistence fund had been available previously which permitted the acquisition of this factor of production. Once this is available, however, it will be available as a lasting aid.

Here it is now necessary to point out that all forms of investment in produced factors of production that can be termed durable can only be considered *relatively durable*. They certainly outlast the individual production process, and further investment will lead to an even larger output. However, every such investment will be used up sometime.[8] Its new creation will only then be possible if a new subsistence fund is available that is sufficient for the length of time needed to carry out the reinvestment. If we perhaps imagine—once again ignoring the synchronization of production—that all production in an economy is structured such that a large subsistence fund initially has made a significant investment in machines ("durable" investments) possible, then the possession of these produced factors of production has continuously permitted an ample provision for the population, and that finally this entire investment is completely worn out and becomes useless. Furthermore, maintaining previous ample provisions for the population is only possible if, in the meantime, a sufficient "renewal fund" has been accumulated; that is, a subsistence fund that provides for the population during the reconstruction of the investment (and during the period of the production of the first products). If this renewal fund is lacking, only a transition to momentary production with its extremely narrow provisions is possible. If the subsistence fund is too small, a transition to methods of production which require smaller amounts of durable factors of production—to a shortening of the roundabout methods of production—is required, which will also bring a lower return.

This rigid model should only illustrate the role of the renewal fund. Maintaining a *continuous* attainment of consumer goods within the framework of a production system that produces durable factors of production in roundabout production methods will only be possible if a corresponding part of the

---

[8]A restriction necessary here will be treated in footnote 13.

product continuously takes over the function of the renewal fund. And with the help of this continuously provided renewal fund, the reacquisition of all of those produced factors of production must be made possible which are needed to replace the used up investments. We shall present a highly stylized example.

In an economy, several factories each produce a specific number of rations of subsistence means (in the broadest sense of the word) every week. For continuous production, the factories require the employment of labor and raw materials which at first are taken directly from nature and are then transformed in other factories. We will assume here that in all of these factories, in those which produce finished consumer goods as well as in those which produce raw materials, there are significant investments of (relatively) durable factors of production. Thus, in addition to a process of current production of means of subsistence, a current production of existing investments in the factories is necessary. We also assume that this takes place in factories which once again employ significant amounts of investment in (the form of) produced factors of production.

The question we ask ourselves is this: How must the regularly reproduced subsistence fund (a specific number of rations of means of subsistence every week) be used so that production can be maintained without interruption? The subsistence fund can only serve to provide for human wants, yet while the subsistence fund is being used up, continuation of production must be made possible in the form of the above-mentioned "reproductive" consumption. It is clear that we must distinguish between different ways in which the subsistence fund is used:

1. The subsistence fund must support everyone who is involved in producing the finished product.

2. The subsistence fund must support everyone who is involved in producing raw materials for the production of means of subsistence.

3. The subsistence fund must support everyone who is involved in the production of machines (relatively durable factors of production); that is, of those machines used directly in the production of consumer goods as well as of those which are used

in the production processes that precede the production of consumer goods.

4. Finally, the subsistence fund must also support everyone who is involved in producing the raw materials used in the machine industry.

Thus, the production of consumer goods must also "support" (*alimentieren*) the creation of durable factors of production and the appropriation of raw materials, i.e., it must supply *these production processes, which themselves produce nothing that can be directly considered consumer goods, with those consumer goods* necessary for the subsistence of those employed in these production processes. Naturally, the form which this support assumes depends on the organization of the economic system. In the case that is relevant to us—a market economy based on division of labor—this process will be in the form of exchanges, such that the owner of a firm producing finished consumer goods first pays from the returns of his production everyone who provides him with originary factors of production for further production, then everyone who supplies him with raw materials, and lastly, everyone who renews his stock of machines. The manufacturer of machines in turn will be able to "work" with the fund he receives from the sale of his produced factors of production. With this fund he in turn pays those who make originary factors of production available to him, those who sell him raw materials, and those who deliver replacements for *used up* machines. In precisely the same way, the producers of raw materials will support their production with that fund of consumption goods which they have attained through the sale of their products. That would be the simplest model. All of these exchange acts can also go through the hands of middlemen. In particular, it will often be possible to smooth over discontinuities by employing middlemen. Thus, perhaps an entrepreneur whose machinery is not yet in need of replacement,[9] but who already continually sets aside a part of his products in order to later be able to "support" the reproduction of his equipment with this renewal fund, will not have to keep this subsistence fund

---

[9]It should be phrased more precisely: for whose renewal no expenditures of labor are necessary as yet. For in general, the process of reproduction in its first stages will have to begin far ahead of the actual moment of demand.

in natura. He can turn it over to someone who will only later return this subsistence fund; and from this point on—since, of course, it is not necessary that the same pieces be returned—this subsistence fund can temporarily (probably in the course of a further exchange) be employed for the purpose of supporting another production process from whose product the timely return to those who originally set aside this subsistence fund in the form of a renewal fund should then be possible. One can also imagine that a subsistence fund is turned over by the consumer goods industry to the preceding production stages of raw materials production for whose output the consumer goods industry only has a demand at a later date. After completion of these preceding production stages, the consumer goods industry will receive the now necessary finished raw materials (or in another case, machines) in place of the renewal fund. Nothing much will change if this process in a monetary economy is finally hidden behind a "veil of money"; if the entrepreneur who builds up a renewal fund does not know that the money he receives in return for his products and deposits in his bank "represents" a subsistence fund; if he who borrows money from the bank is not aware that in so doing he draws from a renewal fund of means of subsistence provided elsewhere in the economy, and that if he pays back the money, he will in turn provide a renewal fund or some products produced with its assistance. Here, however, we will first be concerned with clearly presenting those processes which occur in the realm of real goods.

One must keep in mind that the entire investment of an economy in durable factors of production can only become reproduced with the assistance of a renewal fund, *which originated in the consumer goods industry*, just as the current continuation of the individual production processes from the attainment of raw materials up to the finishing of consumer goods is only possible if the subsistence fund needed for the duration of this process is available. If this last mentioned process corresponds to the example of a production process treated by us earlier, in which a raw material develops into a finished product without producing durable factors of production and a subsistence fund supports this process, then parallel to this process we now see another one in which the reproduction of once-produced equipment takes place and which also must be supported by returns from a subsistence fund. To schematically present the relationships, let the previously discussed model be further elaborated as a numerical example.

Let us assume that out of the return of consumer goods production of 50,000 rations per week, 10,000 are given to laborers employed in the production of consumer goods, an equally large number is given to the suppliers of raw materials, and 30,000 rations form the renewal fund. This renewal fund will be passed on to those production processes which produce the machines employed in the production of consumer goods. Here, it serves in turn the same purpose that the total product serves in the framework of the production of consumer goods: A part (for example, 10,000 rations) will be handed over to the employed laborers, the suppliers of raw materials will receive another part (10,000 rations), and still another part (10,000 rations) will serve in turn as the renewal fund for the reproduction of the equipment used up in this production process. That part of the return from the production of means of subsistence, however, which goes to the producers of raw materials (10,000 rations each, from both the production of consumer goods and the stages of production preceding it), must be handed over again to the just characterized usages. One part (5,000 rations) will be turned over to the employed laborers, while another part (perhaps a greater part, maybe 10,000 rations) is passed on to those who provided the originary factor of production of land, and a last part (5,000 rations) will again have to serve as a renewal fund for the presently employed durable factors of production. For simplicity's sake, we will finally assume here that the renewal of investment in firms producing raw materials as well as in those producing durable factors of production employs originary factors of production exclusively. When we review this process as a whole, we notice that the entire subsistence fund, which is the result of consumer goods production, is assigned to originary factors of production, either directly or indirectly via other production processes. In fact, it will invariably be assigned to factors of production which contribute to the further production of consumer goods, either directly in the production of consumer goods or else in production processes which supply either raw materials or durable factors of production (machines) employed in this production process.[10] Beyond this, however, another thing must be remembered.

The expenditure of an originary factor of production within the framework of roundabout methods of production must—*if production is to be maintained at an unchanged pace*—be reproducible after some time at the same place within the structure of production. And to make this possible, the appropriate ration of the means of subsistence must be available at the correct time to enable the employment of this originary factor of production in a roundabout method of production. Just as the employment of an originary factor of production in roundabout methods of production today is only possible if a ration of a means of subsistence is available to this factor, so will the employment of this factor at the same place in the system of production processes only be possible if today's expenditure of this factor of production for use at a later time has secured the necessary ration of subsistence means. The length of time that passes before the employment of an originary factor of production at the same place within the continuous flow of production again becomes necessary might well vary. In the case of those originary factors of production (laborers) directly employed in the production of consumer goods, a return will soon be the result; under certain circumstances it will occur

---

[10]In this example we have let the originary factors of production which land provides contribute directly and exclusively in the production of raw materials and during the last stage of renewals. It would have been more correct if we had also included such contributions, at least to a small degree (land for factories, etc.), in the other stages of production. We neglected to do this in order not to unduly complicate the presentation. It must be observed, incidentally, when considering the originary contributions of land and soil, that "payment" for such contributions out of the subsistence fund in the form of support for their owners—analogous to the support that must be given to the laborers—cannot be regarded as a necessary prerequisite for roundabout methods of production. This question will be discussed later in a different context. The specifics of the parceling out of the subsistence fund to different stages of the process of production here have been arbitrary. Obviously, the proportions will have to vary drastically depending on the degree of use of durable investments. Let it furthermore be mentioned that with the detailed employment of the return of consumer goods, no claim is being made of having presented a final solution to the problem of apportioning these returns to various production factors. For this reason, we could also ignore the question here whether profits can be made from production which surpass payments for the originary factors of production and the renewal fund.

so quickly that with respect to such factors one cannot even speak of an earlier employment in the production process.[11] For those originary factors that aid in the production of raw materials for the production of consumer goods, one must wait a longer time between their originary employment and the completion of the consumer good. However, all of those originary factors of production employed for the creation of durable factors of production—either directly or indirectly through the expenditure of labor for the production of raw materials needed here—must wait an especially long time until, through the use of these factors of production, consumer goods are created from which a renewal fund can be derived making the reproduction of the previously invested expenditures for the purpose of maintaining the "durable" equipment possible. Regardless of how long this productive contribution is tied up in the roundabout process of production, for every originary factor of production expended, an economic replacement in the form of a finished product must be produced sooner or later. This replacement factor, in order to maintain production, must in turn serve to support an originary factor of production employed at the same place and which, then, again must wait until a new consumer good is produced. It is clear that for this renewed employment of an originary factor of production in the production process, a ration of the subsistence fund must be available in time. Later we will have to handle the question of the quantitative relationship between the factors of production and the product in an expanded framework. Only then will we have to treat the question of a surplus beyond expenditures. Here the problem is different. If a roundabout method of production is to be maintained, then this is only possible such that the same quantities of originary factors of production are always employed and invariably at the same stage of the time-consuming production process. And since in a roundabout process of production a period

---

[11]The baker who produces a finished consumer good daily works in the last stage of a roundabout process of production. In this case, the time that passes from the employment of labor to the attainment of the finished product can for all practical purposes be ignored. (The laborer only receives his wage after the product is completed.) However, it will simplify our presentation here if we assume that in the consumer goods industry, too, support for the laborer results from previously produced consumer goods. This is by no means unrealistic. In particular (more or less) "durable" consumer goods require a longer period of production within the finishing production stage.

of time always passes between the original employment of an originary factor of production and the achievement of an output (for it is only possible to employ factors of production prior to achieving a return if at that point in time a subsistence fund is available), then in order to maintain production, part of its return must be made available for the repetition of the roundabout method of production. Synchronizing production will generally make it possible for an originary factor of production to be reemployed at the same place in a regularly progressing process of production. But one must not take it for granted that this factor of production indeed finds the necessary ration of the available means of subsistence.

Here it was our task to demonstrate that the direction of production towards a timely provision of means of subsistence for each required employment of originary production factors is the precondition for uninterrupted production.

It should be noted that the employment of an originary factor of production in a roundabout method of production always coincides with the expenditure of a ration of subsistence means. It is unimportant whether one says, "We will today expend a certain amount of labor whose return will only be achieved in one year," or "We will today invest a certain number of rations of the subsistence fund which will permit the employment of these laborers." Both are expressions of one and the same process. We can speak of an employment of originary factors of production that occurs prior to the achievement of a product as well as of an investment of rations of means of subsistence, even in the simplest case of a continuous process of production carried out from beginning to end without any durable equipment. We can apply this formula to the case in which on-going production employs large investments of durable factors as well as to the process of producing machines and other durable factors of production. The laborer in the iron ore mine must receive his support as continuously as the laborer in the food industry, the laborer in the machine factory just as the laborer in the weaving industry. All of these expenditures of laborers are expenditures in the roundabout method of production. They would not be possible if a fund of the means of subsistence had not previously been accumulated and is made available for the support of the laborers. Continuous production would not be possible if each time that labor had to be expended at a certain point, a new supply of means of subsistence were not indeed available. It is also clear that only the manifold synchronization of production makes continuous work at all stages of production possible, and that the support of individual labor contributions in the roundabout method of production is only possible insofar as returns of previous production processes are available. Only in the last act of the production of consumer goods, where no significant time elapses between the expenditure of labor and the achievement of the finished product, can an originary factor of production be employed without there previously having been a subsistence fund available for its support.

Wherever originary factors of production serve the purpose of renewing the investment of (relatively) durable factors of production, a renewal fund must be accumulated. We emphasized that such a renewal fund can only be provided by the consumer-goods industry. Wherever a renewal of investments in preceding production stages is necessary, moreover, this renewal is only possible in such a way that the subsistence fund handed over from the consumer goods industry must provide the consumer goods necessary for accomplishing this renewal. A consumer-goods industry equipped with durable factors of production can continue to work for awhile, even if no renewal takes place, if during economic fluctuations the splitting off of a renewal fund out of returns is not possible. Production will then only come to a standstill if the equipment is completely consumed. The production of factors of production is, however, entirely dependent on being supported by a renewal fund provided through the consumer goods industry. It will come to a standstill once no renewal fund is accumulated in production. The renewal fund made available by the consumer goods industry is the economic successor of the expenditures in the production of durable factors of production. The renewed availability of this fund is the precondition for the production of factors of production being able to work towards the renewal of durable investments in the consumer goods industry.

We have demonstrated that for each employment of originary factors of production in the production of durable factors it is necessary in order to maintain production that there be an economic successor in the form of a regenerated subsistence fund, available whenever the time of renewal has come. Only under this condition is a renewed employment of this factor possible. Thus, each expenditure in the process of the creation of factors of production has become fully integrated into our treatment of roundabout methods of production: With every employment of originary factors of production, a subsistence fund must also be present at each stage of the roundabout structure of production. Of course, the situation here is significantly more complicated than in the first model we used, which explained the role of the subsistence fund within the roundabout method of production. The question arises: through what reactions will the economy find its direction in light of this complex structure of the roundabout method of production? Until now it has been our task to explain the way in which production processes must be structured so that a continuous return from production can be expected. We will later expand on this lesson concerning factors of production.

5. Forms of Capital

In analyzing roundabout methods of production, we restricted ourselves to considering relationships in the world of goods. The problem was formulated as such: what is the prerequisite for production's taking advantage of the increased returns associated with choosing roundabout methods of production? We found that the existence of a subsistence fund was this prerequisite. While analyzing roundabout methods of production, we found further that there existed various specific provisions of goods whose production, on the one hand, was the result of choosing roundabout methods of production and whose expenditure, on the other hand, was necessary for the continuation of the roundabout process of production, and which had to be continuously reproduced in order to maintain it. We now wish to consider in summary all of those complexes of goods which we have encountered during our observations. In so doing, we decide to describe them as various forms of capital. But it should once again be pointed out emphatically that we have not the slightest reason here to abandon the greatest possible awareness of the real factors of production. Production employing capital means production using roundabout methods. We are exclusively dealing with occurrences in this realm. Specific features of a monetary economy or features of the socio-economic order are irrelevant here; neither should we assign any role to unrealistic features of an abstract world.

We will now distinguish between three forms of capital:

1. *Free capital*: This is the subsistence fund (supply of consumer goods) which is made available for the support of roundabout methods of production;

2. *Intermediate products*: These are raw materials in the various stages of processing prior to the finishing of the consumer good (raw materials take on the shape of "maturing" consumer goods in the course of processing);

3. *Fixed (stable) capital*: ("relatively durable factors of production": machines, etc.); These are produced factors of production that can be used for a number of individual production processes.

Intermediate products and fixed capital are goods which are characteristic of roundabout methods of production. We will label them with the term "capital goods." In contrast, consumer goods as such are never capital; they only assume the function of capital if they are used in the specific way we previously described with the term "reproductive consumption," i.e., if they serve to support roundabout methods of production. Intermediate products and free capital serve to support the individual production processes and can thus be labeled "liquid" capital in contrast to "fixed" capital. Yet, one must pay attention to the fact that liquid capital is also employed in the process of producing fixed capital.

The production process at work in roundabout methods of production is determined by the employment of these three forms of capital. The fact that originary factors of production can initially be used in the production of intermediate products which mature only in the course of time into finished products, is made possible by a supply of free capital. A special form of roundabout method of production is present if in addition—and this again is only possible under the condition of a supply of free capital—originary factors of production are employed in the production of fixed capital, which later in turn produces the finished product by incorporating intermediate products and additional originary factors of production. However, because the production of a capital good is only possible with the help of a subsistence fund which supports a process that has not yet produced any consumer goods, every capital good must have been preceded by free capital. The capital good is produced as a result of the expenditure of free capital.

Thus, new capital can be formed exclusively by free capital. New capital can only come into existence because finished consumer goods are "saved" and employed so that they permit the choice of a roundabout method of production.[12] This not only applies to the case of building up new capital, intended to increase the economy's supply of capital; it also applies to the renewal of all capital that has been invested in the economy. Every roundabout process of production begins with the investment of free capital, and every further step in the production process implies a new expenditure of free capital. The period of time this free capital is tied up will vary in length, and the form of the capital goods that result from the tying up of free capital will vary too, depending on whether durable capital goods are produced or the investment leads to intermediate products. In both cases, however, the tying up of capital is only temporary, and the once saved and then invested free capital will later be set "free" again in the form of consumer goods. If production is to be maintained, this freed capital

---

[12]The doctrine regarding roundabout methods of production leads to the wage-fund theory via this thesis: employing originary factors of production in a roundabout method of production is not possible without assuring the support of the same. We have seen that a wage fund must have been accumulated in advance or must have been provided for out of the returns of another production process. The following must be said here regarding a possible objection: Let us assume that the fishermen in Roscher's example accumulate their capital by reducing their consumption and only use half a day to catch fish, while they use the rest of their working day to produce capital goods. An integration into our model is easily possible here. We distinguish between two parallel production processes: The consumer goods produced in one also serve to support the other roundabout production process. It is decisive that here, too, the possibility of roundabout methods of production is dependent on support. This applies also in the case in which a supplementation of the wage fund through a reduction in consumption occurs or, as we will later formulate, the "virulent" nature of the subsistence fund is increased by reducing the rations in which it is consumed.

must in turn be incorporated into the roundabout method of production. It must "support" the employment of originary factors of production in a time-consuming roundabout method of production. If this does not happen, production must be discontinued during the next production period.[13] If the roundabout production process is to be repeated, then the once-saved free capital must continue to function as capital after it is freed from its temporary binding in an intermediate product or in a fixed capital investment. In this regard, G. Akerman coined the particularly appropriate phrase "maintained savings": In order to maintain the continuous provisions generated through time-consuming production processes, it does not suffice that one once saved. It is equally critical that the free capital invested in production—regardless of whether it has been transformed into an intermediate product or into fixed capital investments—is reinvested after its release.

---

[13] If we assume that all invested capital must necessarily be set free and that a repetition of each expenditure of capital is necessary, then we are thereby considering basically only one part of the process of expending capital. There are also investments in which a repetition of capital expenditure is not necessary; this is probably the case in some kinds of land and soil improvements. Here a one-time expenditure of capital can make these originary factors of production available in a better form once and for all. A particularly instructive example is the removal of a boulder obstructing the cultivation of a field. The one-time investment of capital provides a continuous increase in profits. We will not treat such cases further and will only point out here that if a market rate of interest exists, such expenditures can easily be incorporated into profit accounting based on their expected surplus return. In addition, a second case deserves attention here: that in which the initial expenditure of capital is greater than those expenditures that will later be necessary to maintain the factors. Again, certain soil improvements may be cited as an example. Obviously, the comparison here between initial capital expenditures and the size of the "maintenance contribution," which takes the place of the renewal fund, is only possible via a calculation of interest. The characterization of forms of capital employment presented in the text probably corresponds to the more important cases. We need them in order to be able to analyze the conditions for the process of a "static" (in the sense of stationary) economy. Such an economic process must bring about the continual renewal of the same investment expenditures. To formulate the conditions for this economic process is simultaneously to formulate the prerequisites for the fact that some specific return from production can be attained over and over again; thus there are, so to speak, minimum requirements to be formulated whose fulfillment prevents an impoverishment of the economy. In this process, one-time investments which need not be renewed in full cannot be included. The static process implies that each expenditure must be repeated, and it is our task to formulate the prerequisites necessary for such repetitions. Contrary to this task, the question of non-repeatable investments is of no significance for us.

Each time free capital is tied up, a more or less extensive restriction in the possible employments for this capital is implied. Free capital can be assigned to every possible use in roundabout methods of production. However, if free capital is used, for example, to produce iron ("invested" in this capital good), then the range for its further use is reduced. It is still possible that this iron may develop from an intermediate product into a finished consumer good (for example, an automobile[14]), or to use it for the production of a machine—fixed capital. The machine can sometimes have a very wide range of uses (a simple lathe and even the most simple tools are examples here), but it can also be designed for very specific uses (a complex textile machine), and otherwise be practically useless. Thus, in the course of production, free capital assumes a more or less "specific"[15] form, so that only a narrow range of uses remains open.

The process of transforming free capital into capital goods which frequently have a highly specific nature and which always have a more restricted range of uses than free capital is of the greatest importance whenever there is a question of reemploying tied up capital in different production processes. This is important for two reasons: First, the transfer of capital from one production process into another can be problematic whenever an error in the direction of production has led to producing too much

---

[14]The durable "consumer good" should actually not even be classified as a consumer good in the strictest sense of the word. What is consumed here are the "use values" embodied in a desirable consumer good. It would be more appropriate to classify this as a durable capital good which often—but not always, as for example, a house or an automobile—makes its use values available for consumption without requiring additional factors of production. This view, though, faces the difficulty that even today one all too readily holds onto a "materialistic or objectivistic interpretation" of goods. Yet, if the durable consumer good is conceived of as a capital good, then its incorporation into the problem of renewal can be accomplished easily. "Static" maintenance of a house, for example, requires the steady splitting off of a renewal fund from returns. In the following we will no longer concern ourselves with the question of durable consumer goods. From this viewpoint, further lengthening of roundabout production methods would probably have to be assumed if better, more durable consumer goods are produced. (Böhm-Bawerk speaks in this regard of an "important parallel development of capitalist roundabout methods of production.")

[15]This expression follows Wieser's terminology as used by Hayek.

of one kind of a consumer good and too little of another, such that production does not reflect demand. Second, it can become a problem that free capital has been invested in too lengthy of roundabout methods of production, such that the result is a production structure for which, along with too many capital goods, there is too little free capital. In both cases, the fact that capital goods that have assumed a specific form are not employed and other goods are required in their place—in the second case, consumer goods instead of capital goods or, in the first, different capital goods rather than the actually available ones—will lead to difficulties because the specific quality of the capital goods makes a reallocation difficult.

The notion of the liquidity of capital investments as a problem of capital formation arises from the fact that free capital invested in capital goods cannot perform the same function as free capital. The length of time free capital is tied up will be the shortest for free capital used to employ originary factors of production in the production of consumer goods. It will be longer when free capital supports originary factors in the production of raw materials. It will be longest when free capital is used to direct originary factors of production into the production of durable capital goods. If an excessive investment of capital has taken place, then investments in the economy certainly exist which might later permit the production of means of subsistence, but the thing lacking right now is free capital which permits the continuation of production. This situation can be described most precisely with the formula that every capital good, and in particular every durable capital good, requires a corresponding amount of free capital in the form of a *complementary good* if it is to aid in supporting the economy.[16] If capital investment does not find the necessary complements of free capital, then a "disproportionality" in the structure of proportions exists: Free capital is "misdirected" in that it has been invested to too great an extent in equipment

---

[16]The doctrine of complementary goods was developed by Menger. An exception to the above presented principle would only be at hand if one is concerned with capital goods which are so close to the consumable state that without a—here relevant—loss of time they can be turned into finished consumer goods. For the general considerations presented here regarding the liquidity of capital investments, these exceptions need not be of further concern.

without enough free capital having been made available to make the completion of production possible.

If one wishes to emphasize that here the free capital has been tied up, one might say that capital has been immobilized, that capital investments have become illiquid. Stated simply: The machines and raw materials are there, but there is too little of that which the people who work need for their subsistence; the workers cannot work in advance of their payment if they have nothing to live on. Free capital is normally used such that it again becomes "liquid" free capital after it has been tied up for some time. In the case of immobilization, however, capital has been excessively directed into uses from which it cannot be freed up in time, and hence cannot be freed at all. For the only way to free up capital that has once been tied up (invested) is to carry out the once-begun roundabout production until it is completed: Only when a product becomes a consumer good is the once tied up capital free again. It is clear that an excessive tying up of free capital is identical to the choice of too lengthy roundabout methods of production. For the "correct" length of the roundabout methods of production exists whenever the roundabout methods of production are extended as far as the available supply of free capital permits without there being a reduction in the supply of products.[17] If the normal process of liquidating capital investments—a continuation of the planned production—cannot be carried out due to a lack of free capital, then it will be necessary to shorten the roundabout methods of production. If the population did not realize in time that too lengthy a roundabout method of production had been chosen, and if it consumed and invested[18] the free capital without

---

[17]The choice of too-short roundabout methods of production will result in a situation in which the advantage of extending the roundabout method of production—increased returns—is not reached. This will manifest itself in excessive liquidity, i.e., in an especially abundant supply of free capital, which contrasts with lower future production returns. We will have more to say about this situation later.

[18]Consume and invest are identical here: insofar as free capital (a subsistence fund) serves to support factors of production at work in a roundabout method of production which does not yet generate consumable products, this free capital serves simultaneously to support those who provide the originary factors of production. Consumption would only be a separate concept from investment insofar

assuring its timely reproduction; and if half-finished products but not consumer goods were thus available to the population, then each roundabout production process would have to be discontinued and production would have to take on the form of momentary production. We have already pointed this out. In fact, it will not have to come to this for two reasons. First, the state of immobilized capital will probably be noticed before it actually arises. In such a case, production will be transformed such that part of the roundabout methods of production will be discontinued while another part will be continued with the help of an increased addition of originary factors of production which are supported by the rest of the available free capital; this is equivalent to shortening the roundabout method in such lines of production.[19] Second, however, a transformation of production—again in the sense of shortening the roundabout production process—will be possible by transferring capital goods that have an unspecific nature from a longer planned roundabout method of production to a shorter one. To the extent that this is possible, capital goods which are the result of an excessive lengthening of roundabout methods of production can still be usefully employed. Sometimes, however, a loss of investments

---

as the means of subsistence do not support "reproductive consumption." Yet, this has been excluded by the definition of free capital. It only includes those means of subsistence used to support originary factors of production.

[19]If free capital in the amount of n is available but the continuation of the entire production process requires $2n$, then the continuation of half the production with the addition of free capital in the amount of n; that is, the addition of relatively more originary factors of production in the next production period, means shortening the roundabout methods of production in these lines as compared to the situation where the capital already invested here can be employed with only half of the liquid capital n; for then relatively more originary factors of production are employed in a stage of the production process closer to the finished product. (This could also be illustrated by the well-known method of calculating averages. The average length of time capital is tied up in a production would have to be contrasted with the longest period of time that passes between the expenditure of a factor of production and the repetition of the same expenditure. The first magnitude could serve as an index for the capital intensity of production, while the second would determine the length of the time period within which production expenditures must be repeated in the course of a static economy.)

will be associated with such reallocations. This shall be discussed later in a different connection.[20]

It was our task here to clarify the role of capital in production. We have seen that the function of capital is determined exclusively by the fact that roundabout production is only possible if a subsistence fund is available to support those who supply originary factors of production. *All problems of capital can be deduced from this.* In particular, capital invested in durable factors of production must never be considered as separate from the problem of roundabout processes of production. If one wished to begin with the fact that there are physical goods which aid in production and help increase it, one could never solve the task that one faces from an economic point of view. For these capital investments, too, are intimately connected with the problem of roundabout methods of production by two factors. First, even the most durable capital investment can only be considered relatively durable, and thus necessarily requires for its maintenance a steadily renewed expenditure of originary factors of production which must be invested long before they can attain a return of consumer goods. These expenditures which are only possible if, as for any roundabout method of production, free capital is available. Closely related to this is the fact that durable capital must provide a renewal fund of free capital out of its returns if it is to be maintained. And second, there is a relationship between durable capital investments and the problem of roundabout production processes because durable capital investments always require free capital as a complementary good. Clearly, the supplementation of fixed capital with free capital that remains tied up for an especially long time is necessary wherever the length of time that passes between the employment of the capital investment and the production of consumer goods is as long as will be the case for investments in the production

---

[20]There would be a third possibility of "stretching" the available subsistence fund by shortening the rations in which it is used up in supporting originary factors of production. With this the possibility of beginning a longer roundabout method of production with the available subsistence fund would emerge. We will disregard this possibility here—as previously—because we wish to treat the question of the size of the rations later when we discuss the formation of the prices of factors of production within the framework of an analysis of a market economy.

goods industry—whereas wherever the fixed capital investment serves directly to produce consumer goods, there will be a noticeably smaller demand for free capital for a shorter binding period. In fact, under certain circumstances the importance of free capital will be reduced entirely. But even here there is a connection with a need for free capital, and indeed, an indirect demand for free capital will be particularly great because these investments can only be maintained by means of continuous renewal. Such renewal is only possible by maintaining the entire preceding production of factors of production which requires large amounts of free capital and capital that must be tied up for a long period of time.

In explaining the principles which generally guide production in roundabout methods, we have so far avoided asking how economic forces manage to adapt production to these principles. When we saw that production must adjust the length of the roundabout methods of production to the supply of free capital, we did not ask how this adjustment will take place. The general law that the choice of too short a roundabout method of production must forgo a possible increase in production and that the choice of too lengthy a roundabout method of production must lead to an immobilization of the economy's supply of capital says nothing about how the adjustment of production to the supply of capital will occur. We will only later treat these questions within the framework of our discussion of the formation of prices in a market economy. Only then will we see that what determines all adjustments of production processes to the supply of capital is the height of the interest rate.

THE VERTICAL AND HORIZONTAL CONNECTIVITY OF PRICES

1. The Price System

The market process moves between two poles: the supply of factors of production and the demand for consumer goods. Insofar as this process is solely determined by the principle of exchanging real goods (including labor expenditures), the people demanding consumer goods and the people providing factors of production are necessarily identical. No economic subject can obtain a consumer good from the exchange economy who has not supplied a factor of production in return—thus the image of a circulation within the economy. The individual owners of factors of production make them available to the economic process and receive in exchange consumer goods. Insofar as the owners of factors of production (laborers) are dependent for their economic existence on attaining a return from their labors, it simultaneously becomes possible for them to continue to take part in the economic process, to again supply their factors of production, and to repeatedly obtain a share of the products. There is, of course, no reason to assume that this economic circulation will display a perennial repetition of one and the same process. Even if an economic actor repeatedly makes his factors of production available in order to attain a share of the product, within the fluctuations of the economy it can always happen that, on the one hand, the factors of production an individual owns change or, on the other hand, that the share he receives of the returns from the economic process changes, even if his supply of factors of production remains the same. There can be various reasons for such changes which we cannot treat in detail here. For certain reasons, however, it will now be necessary for us to attempt to explain the course of the economic process independently of such possible changes. Only in this way will it be possible for us to accurately describe two far-reaching and important principles of economic processes which are strict laws in the framework of such a "static" economy[21] while, if one enriches the picture of the economy by including such changes and brings it closer to reality, they only have an effect as "tendencies." Nonetheless, the significance of these principles, even if they only appear as tendencies, justifies that we now grant more space to their rigorous derivation.

For factors of production as well as for products, prices will develop on the market; and in an exchange economy, the more the process of employing factors of production to produce consumer goods is divided in horizontal and vertical directions (whereby the various partial production processes are interconnected through exchanges), the greater will be the number of prices which develop in the market. In a free market, the formation of each of these prices is determined by the intersection of supply and demand. The principles that are valid here are presented in the general law of prices. Here we are satisfied with the most general formulation: If the supply is structured such that it increases with increasing prices, while the demand decreases with increasing prices, then there can only be one price at which the supply is equal to demand. With free competition on both sides, the "economic selection principle of price rivalry" will determine the price height. In addition, a necessary connectivity of various prices will be noted, a connectivity so tight that all prices appear as a single system in which each individual price is dependent on every other. For one thing, there is a connectivity of prices in a vertical direction; that is, there exists a connection between the prices of products and the prices of factors of production that has been expressed by the law of costs. Second, a connectivity of prices also exists in a horizontal direction. It results

---

[21]Here this means the following: Consider a "stationary" economic system, i.e., an economic process in which the same steps are always repeated. With this, a constancy in the data is assumed. A further assumption, however, which shall not be further explained here, must be made regarding the temporal integration of economic goals: The economic subjects must desire a stable provision for the present and the future. We will have more to say about this later.

from the fact that various goods can replace each other in the economic process and be reallocated from one use to another. This relationship has been expressed by the principle of substitution.

It is important here that this principle of the connectivity of prices be related clearly to the general principle of price formation. Since every price formation in the free market can only be explained in terms of supply and demand, the horizontal and vertical connectivity of prices can only result from the fact that the supply of and demand for a good are dependent in some way on the prices of all other goods. The doctrine of the connectivity of prices is thus essentially a doctrine of the determinateness of specific supply and demand configurations. It will have to be shown that under certain circumstances, regardless of the existence of a price that equilibrates supply and demand of a good, supply and demand of this good will have to change because of the relationship between this price and other prices. It should be clear from the beginning that here one will be dealing with the supply and demand of products.

Let us point out briefly that for economic theory, the transition from viewing isolated price formations to viewing the connectivity of prices implies fulfilling the requirement of being systematic. This is the only possible way of analyzing the economy as a whole. Individual movements are exclusively formations of single prices determined by supply and demand, and only when it is possible to trace these movements in all their effects until a picture emerges in which each phenomenon is co-determined by every other, and in which the law-governed nature of the whole follows from the determining forces of each part, is the task of presenting the entire economic cosmos fulfilled. It is the duty of every science to create a coherent system. To fulfill this task means, however, to hammer this system out of the laws determining its parts.

2. The Supply of Factors of Production

Regarding the supply of factors of production, it must first be pointed out that it would be misguided to consider only the two originary factors of production, land and labor, and produced factors of production (capital goods), and to overlook the fact that in each of these three groups of factors of production very different supplies exist side by side. Even in considering the factor of labor, it is very clear that one should never speak of labor as such, but that labor services of varying quality exist. The same is true regarding nature. Here, land serves as the foremost aid in the production of agricultural products (as farmland), but also—particularly in considering urban development—as the standing room for residential housing and work places, and finally, as provider of all raw materials, natural sources of energy and transportation, etc. Since the problem of employing land and the formation of prices for its use does not interest us as a special problem, in the following discussion for the sake of simplicity we are only considering the employment of land as it is used agriculturally. However, even regarding land used for farming there is a great difference in quality. Finally, with respect to capital it is clear that in addition to the subsistence fund which can be viewed as free capital, there is a supply of very different kinds of produced factors of production; we will speak of this supply in particular later.

Here it is necessary to point out this generally known fact in order to first show that along with the question of the formation of the prices of factors of production there also arises the question of a variety of other prices. In some cases, different kinds of factors of production can be substituted for others without complications because a quantity of one equals a quantity of another in terms of productive services. In many cases, however, this substitution will take place with greater or lesser difficulties. Such a substitution—and it is important that one recognizes this from the very beginning—will also be possible between factors of production of different kinds, as the most simple example of substituting machines for human labor illustrates. For now, however, we will prefer to consider the supply of different kinds of factors of production in complete "isolation." We will thus arrive at a large number of supply curves, each of which will be relatively restricted.

Regarding all of these supply curves, we will start with the assumption that each has the shape which we already chose as our point of departure in explaining the general law of prices, i.e., that the supply will be greater the higher the price is that can be obtained in the market. Naturally, it is of no importance here whether only a great increase in price effects an increase in supply, or whether this is already accomplished with a slight increase in price. Thus, the supply curve in the usual graphic presentation can approach a vertical as well as a horizontal shape. It is only a prerequisite that an increase in price cannot lead to a decrease in supply. We will have more to say about the justification for this assumption later.

As far as the supply of land is concerned, there are no difficulties. The supply curve will run horizontally, or almost horizontally with only a weak upward slope. The latter is the case insofar as individual land owners do not make their land available for production because prices are too low, and they instead prefer to hold their land in reserve. In contrast, as far as the supply of labor is concerned, under certain circumstances a falling supply curve is conceivable. It is possible, for example, that with increasing wages, laborers who have already reached their desired standard of living, or laborers who share in another's income (housewives), refrain from additional work despite higher wages. For similar reasons—and this is perhaps even more important in practice—the labor supply can increase with falling wages: the laborers work more to maintain their previous standard of living; despite falling wages, laborers' wives go to work if the family's standard of living has become too low because of the husband's reduced earnings. Such possibilities shall first be excluded from consideration. We will only later be able to see that in such cases there is always a situation which lies outside the scope of the static economy considered here. Let it, however, be pointed out that important social forces will tend to stratify the supply of individual labor so as to take on the form of an upward sloping supply curve. This can be understood easily if one considers the meaning of the individual units which compose the aggregate labor supply. Indeed, this supply curve is supposed to display the lowest wage that an individual laborer is prepared to accept as compensation for his work. When the laborer enters the labor market in order to sell his labor services, he wants to find the greatest possible return. Because the individual desperately needs such returns in order to support himself, in extreme cases a large majority of laborers will be prepared to go to work for very low wages. Yet, there will also be a number of laborers for whom this social pressure will be somewhat lower and who hence will only be prepared to take on the strain ("disutility") of work for higher wages. This stratification of social pressure burdening individual workers to different degrees will apparently be highly varied. Let it be noted, for instance, that the head of the family will generally be under greater pressure and hence, will be prepared in the most extreme case to go to work for an even lower wage than the youth or independent laborer who can find support among relatives or who can find employment (at least occasionally) outside of the normal labor market. All sorts of motivations will play a role in shaping the supply of labor. Thus, occasionally the laborer who has some reserves will withhold his supply if the pressure on wages is increased. On the other hand, the laborer who desires to increase his savings will accept even drastically reduced wages to avoid drawing down his reserves. Yet even among individual laborers, the desire to maintain a traditional minimum wage will assume different importance, and in particular—again depending on the degree of social pressure borne by each individual—an acceptance of lowered wages will occur sooner or later for different individuals. The argument we have presented here which shows a "stratification" of the labor supply shall be the center of the following "static analysis" of the labor supply. The great social significance of such stratification for those providing labor services is clear. With sinking wages, those laborers will first give up work for whom supplying labor is least "urgent," who are only prepared to work for a higher wage, while he who is subject to more severe social pressure and hence is willing to work for a lower wage will remain employed. On the other hand, with an increased demand for labor, the necessity of attracting workers who were only prepared to work for a higher wage will also raise the wage for the other suppliers of labor. This all holds true for each individual group of laborers. However, insofar as a sharp increase in demand also requires the attraction of laborers from different groups and thus must take account of entirely different supply curves, in this case, too, an expansion of the supply of labor will only be possible by increasing wages. This applies to attracting laborers from different occupations and geographically separated labor markets, insofar as in both cases there was previously no smooth communication. Generally, it can probably be assumed that in practice the supply curve of labor is shaped such that after an increase from a very low level over a relatively long period, it runs almost horizontally in order to then slope upwards steeply. We will base our considerations initially on the assumption that the supply curve of labor has this form.

Regarding the supply of capital, let nothing further be said here. It is clear that with respect to the supply of capital goods, the issue of the supply of products as an already "derived" supply will have to be taken into consideration.

3. The Supply and Demand of Entrepreneurs. The Law of Costs

The entrepreneur purchases factors of production and sells their product to his buyers. Clearly, no entrepreneur will carry out production from which the revenue is less than the cost of purchasing the factors of production. This obvious fact only becomes worthy of closer consideration because a situation is at hand here which opens up a path towards understanding the problem of the employment of all factors of production. Thus, here in particular it will be necessary to begin by considering the most elementary cases in order to describe precisely the conditions that determine the role of the entrepreneur as demander of factors of production as well as supplier *vis-à-vis* demanding purchasers—whether these be consumers or buyers of intermediate products. We had the opportunity earlier to point out that the determination of demand and supply curves becomes an issue here.

The situation will be an extremely simple one if we imagine that the entrepreneur only requires one single (originary) factor of production in his production process. So as not to have to speak in completely abstract terms, we would like to present an example here with respect to which it might be noted that such a simplistic situation will only rarely occur today. Yet the range of possible examples is not too large, and one must be satisfied with being able to find a somewhat arbitrarily construed example if this can be used in our case without strong objections. We will thus assume that in a mid-sized town there are a number of entrepreneurs who are in the business of house-cleaning. They employ laborers and see to it that residences are cleaned by these workers.[22] On the one hand, the entrepreneurs are faced with a demand for their services, but it is clear that if the prices for these services increase, the demand will decrease—the housewives will then either carry out the cleaning themselves or restrict their use of the service. On the other hand, the entrepreneurs are faced with a relatively limited supply of cleaning women which will clearly remain low if wages are too low, yet in a mid-sized town a significantly greater demand can only be satisfied with increased wages. It is easy to see that the entrepreneurs' demand for laborers will be determined by the demand of "consumers" for the services offered by the entrepreneur. The entrepreneur will not be able to take on any job for which he does not receive at least his cost for labor wages; moreover he will strive for a profit for himself and will probably not take on work without expecting to achieve such a profit. However, the entrepreneur will also not be able to make an "excessive profit" under free competition because otherwise another entrepreneur could be cheaper and would be able to take away work from him. Every entrepreneur would have an interest in attaining a greater profit by expanding his operations. A uniform market price will arise for wages as well as for the entrepreneur's services, and finally, so to say, also for the entrepreneurs' profits. The "mechanism" of the law of cost in the free market can be seen clearly in our example:

A. If the price for an entrepreneur's service is a loss price, then the entrepreneurs will:

1. cease to serve those least able to pay for their services and only satisfy those more able to pay by raising their prices; however, they will also

2. discharge part of their employees and lower wages such that only the "cheaper" laborers remain employed, thereby lowering costs.

---

[22]That there is no production in a technical sense here may not be an objection. The choice of this example should make it possible to abstract from the employment of several different kinds of factors of production (here we can ignore the "material"), and further, to ignore the so-called "advance payment" of wages by the entrepreneur, i.e., the payment of wages before the completion of the product in time-consuming roundabout methods of production.

Both tendencies—raising the price for the product as well as lowering cost—will complement each other. The movement will come to a standstill at the point at which the cost (including the entrepreneur's profit) is equal to the price of the service offered by the entrepreneur.

B. If the price of the entrepreneur's service is significantly above cost, then the entrepreneurs will:

1. see that by expanding their supply they will make additional profits, and the expansion of the supply will force the price down;

2. need more laborers and will only be able to attract them at higher wages.

Again, both of these tendencies—lowering the price of the product and raising the cost—will converge, and the movement will only come to a standstill when a situation is reached where costs (including the entrepreneur's profits) are equal to the price of the service.

This convergence of two price magnitudes is not at all to be considered a "middle line." It is clear that the movement—precisely as in the most simple case of a price formation on the free market—is a movement along two curves which must intersect. Hence, it is also obvious that it depends on the shape of the two curves, on their slope, whether the quantitative change will be a large one and whether the price of the entrepreneur's service or the price of the cost-items will change dramatically. The entire process of adjustment to the law of costs means, however—and it is important to emphasize this again—nothing but a transformation of supply and demand curves. Let us consider the case in which losses have occurred. Here there is an equilibrium on the market in which the labor services are demanded as well as on the market in which the entrepreneurs' services are offered. The entrepreneurs have demonstrated a certain demand for labor, and this has been satisfied according to the given supply of labor. Simultaneously, the entrepreneurs have brought a supply of their services onto the market and this has been accepted by those demanding the service who are most able to pay. The law of costs has not yet come into effect, but on both markets in which prices have formed, this has occurred according to the general law of price formation. According to the law of costs, however, the relationship between these two prices was not correct, and this circumstance forces the entrepreneurs to change their position as demanders of labor as well as suppliers of services. The entrepreneurs must revise their position as suppliers and demanders. Under the influence of losses they must recognize that at the wages paid until now, they can no longer employ as many laborers as before. Their demand has changed, and at the prevailing prices they can no longer offer so many services; hence, their supply has changed.

The function of entrepreneurs under the effectiveness of the law of costs and free competition has been made clear: They obtain the supply of factors of production and compare it to the demand of consumers, or—which is essentially the same thing—they obtain the demand of the consumers and compare it to the supply of factors of production. Whether the entrepreneurs appear as suppliers or as demanders, they must adjust the structuring of their supply and demand to constraints arising from the fact that they only function as middlemen.

It was our task here to present the relationship dealt with by the law of costs in their simplest form. One must not forget these relationships if one proceeds to consider reality in its more complex forms.

4. Complementary Factors of Production. The "Law of Diminishing Returns" and the Principle of Marginal Productivity

Of the simplifications that we just assumed in deriving the law of costs, the most important one was that the entrepreneur employed only one single factor of production. Even the example of the entrepreneur in the house-cleaning business was hardly an accurate description of reality. Wherever technical production processes are carried out, it will have to be assumed that several factors of production are used next to one another. If we now incorporate the use of "complementary goods" as factors into our previous account of the law of costs, then the essence of the problem we are faced with can be summed up easily. In the market for individual factors of production, prices have been formed based on the supply of the owners of factors of production and the demand of entrepreneurs, and these prices appear in the entrepreneur's cost calculations. The average total cost must be compared to the price of the product, and the mechanism of the law of costs will have to bring about an adjustment. While we said before that the entrepreneur takes on the demand of the consumers and relates this demand to a single production factor, in the case of several co-existing factors of production the problem arises of how to break down the uniform consumer demand for the product into a multitude of demand curves for various individual factors of production. In short, the question is how to break down one demand into a multitude of demands. Closely related to this question is a second question which arises from the interaction of a multitude of factors of production. Generally, in combining several factors of production in one production process the situation will not be such that these factors of production will only be able to be employed in one uniform, unchangeable combination. Instead, it is almost always the case that the productive combination can be varied so that one of the factors of production can be utilized in a greater quantity to the disadvantage of others, but also that a factor of production can be completely dispensed with and replaced by another that previously had not been used. Thus, in addition to the problem of breaking down demand, the problem of substituting factors of production arises. Both problems can only be solved together.

Let it be noted that we thus find ourselves confronted with one of the central problems of an economy. If one must begin by assuming the existence of factors of production and consumer demand, then now the question is how the factors of production are employed. Whether a factor of production shall be part of one or another production process, whether it will produce one or another consumer good, whether more will be produced of one or another consumer good and will be made available to the consumers, whether the owners of individual factors of production receive much or little for their contribution to the economic process, even whether one or another factor of production is used at all; all of this becomes an issue here. The decisive function of every question related to the law of costs in determining the economic process is clear. It is no wonder, then, that the questions themselves requiring such far-reaching answers will also cause some difficulties. However, economic theory has found a tool which makes possible an extremely simple solution to the problem. Perhaps what matters today is merely that it be used in a correct way, and not lead to distorting reality. The principle is the law of marginal productivity.

Let us assume that of several different factors of production—for example two, although it could be any number—several units are employed in a production process, and let us assume, given a specific combination of these factors of production, that for one of them the number of employed units is increased or decreased. It will then be possible to find a specific relationship between such variations and the size of the return from production that is expressed in the law of diminishing returns. We will discuss this relationship by first considering its most simple formula, the so-called law of diminishing returns from agricultural production.

An increase in labor expenditures on a given piece of soil can bring about an increase in returns, yet this increase in returns is not necessarily proportionate to the addition of labor expenditure, but instead lags behind. *This follows with necessity from the fact that one is concerned here exclusively with economic goods.* If the law of diminishing returns were not valid, and thus if a doubling of, say, labor expenditures, brought about a doubling of returns, then no farmer would desire an increase in his land holdings for economic reasons, and hence he would not be prepared to pay anything to increase his land in order to produce a larger return. For doubling his acreage while simultaneously doubling the labor expenditures would only result in a doubling of the output; yet if the law of diminishing returns were not true, this doubled return would already be possible by doubling the labor expenditures with the given land. If, however, a doubling of the acreage appears desirable to every farmer in our economy, and if every farmer knows that for this doubling of acreage a payment is justified, then it follows that in doubling the land and simultaneously doubling labor efforts, more can be produced than by solely doubling labor efforts without doubling land. On the other hand, if the law of diminishing returns were not true, a reduction of land by half, too, would be irrelevant, since the same expenditure on half as much land would imply that on this amount of land the labor expenditure had been doubled. If his doubling of labor expenditures brought about a doubling of returns, the farmer could turn over half of his land without hesitation.[23]

If one represents this relationship in the familiar graphic model, then each increase in return associated with an additional laborer employed on a given piece of land is depicted such that each laborer, represented on the X-axis, is related to an increase in output, represented by a narrow rectangle. Each additional laborer produces an increase in output which will become smaller with each addition. With each given number of laborers, the marginal product of labor is to be measured by the output of the last employed laborer or by the loss of output caused by the loss of such a laborer.

Before we continue, however, it will be necessary to extend the argument to the generally valid law of marginal productivity. In our derivation we also could have spoken of factors of production in general instead of land and labor. This is obvious from the fact that in the case of diminishing agricultural returns, we could simply reverse the roles of labor and land. There is also no reason to assume that the principle of diminishing returns is valid only for the use of soil and land as a factor of production. What makes the "law of diminishing returns" so vivid in the case of land is only the accidental circumstance that apparently a strongly diverse intensity of utilization, i.e., the employment of more or less labor, is possible here and that this unrestricted variability of factors of production, especially with regard to a continuous increase or decrease in returns brought about by adding or subtracting a complementary factor, can be imagined without difficulty. The situation appears to be different if one considers a modern machine in combination with other factors of production. With a modern cigarette machine, for instance, by adding more labor and more raw materials an increase in the output will

---

[23]Here we could also have spoken of an increase in any other proportion rather than doubling a cooperating factor of production. See on this the explanations on pages 85ff.

only be possible if the daily work time is lengthened.[24] According to the law of diminishing returns, an increase in returns beyond this will not be possible. Likewise, a reduction in the expenditure of labor and raw materials will shorten the output linearly because the machines will operate for a shorter time daily. The marginal product of labor could not be registered there at all. But even this difficulty can be overcome. One must only be able to rid oneself of a purely technological perspective. Let us regard the cigarette machine as a product of iron and human labor—whereby we must not yet consider the peculiarities resulting from the time consuming roundabout method of production. The actual machine we see can, of course, not be retransformed into the factors of production from which it was created. But this is insignificant. Let us consider the problem as it appears when considering the general law of marginal productivity. Instead of the combination of labor and iron resulting in a machine that can only be combined with a specific amount of labor, a different sort of combination shall be considered. Less iron and less "previous" labor, but more "current" labor shall be employed. If we pose the problem in this way, a solution to the question of the marginal productivity of labor is possible. From the most primitive production of rolling and filling the cigarette by hand to the most modern automats, all conceivable combinations of iron, previous labor, and current labor are possible. We are faced with endless possible combinations of factors of production. From whatever "cleverly chosen"[25] combination we wish to proceed, we would always see that the increase of one of these factors of production brings about an increase in output, but that the return cannot grow in the same proportion as this one factor of production. Only a parallel increase of all factors of production can result in a proportional increase in output. Based on this argument, the principle of marginal productivity can be applied to every factor of production.

It is now clear that with this explanation of the law of marginal productivity we have avoided a number of significant

---

[24]To a limited extent perhaps also by speeding up the tempo of the machine.

[25]We will still see that a combination of freely movable factors of production, such that the increase of one factor of production brings an increasing return, can have no place in a rational economic plan.

problems. Even regarding the example of the cigarette machine one could make objections. If a factory has a number of machines, then the loss of one laborer after another always means an equivalent loss of products. If half of the laborers leave, then half of the machines will have to remain idle and only half of the products can be produced. No connection that would correspond to the law of diminishing returns can be observed here; the calculation of a marginal product of labor is completely impossible. Beyond this, however, additional objections could arise. Today one hears only too often of cases in which the increase in one factor of production can bring about an overproportional increase in returns. A factory in which significant expenditures are necessary in order to prepare for a production process will be able to increase its returns over-proportionally by expanding production from a very low production level by means of a relatively minor expansion in its expenditures for additional factors of production. The "law of increasing returns" will apply. We will not be able to tackle such cases in detail until later. The path along which we indicated the solution to this problem in the example of the cigarette machine will also lead us to a clarification. In essence, it will always be that production can be organized so that it takes advantage of the principle of marginal productivity, and production which is not so adjusted must prove to be misled in some way. This will be discussed later. Here, however, we want to arrive at a final consideration of the law of costs in which we will work solely with the principle of marginal productivity.

The problem of breaking down different demands *vis-à-vis* the supply of individual factors of production is solved with one stroke by using the principle of marginal productivity: The demand for an individual product unit is faced with the supply of individual factor units. Every increase in products does not mean an increase in all factors of production that are employed in a productive combination, but rather an increase of one or another factor of production. The entrepreneur will compare the demand for factors of production which signify possible production and a possible sale of a product with the supply of various individual factors of production, and will do business with the owner of a factor of production who makes him the best offer.

Each factor of production whose marginal product can obtain a price larger than the price of this factor will be employed up to the point at which these two prices are equal. And similarly, of each factor of production that costs more than the price of its marginal product, individual units will no longer be employed. This process will continue until a price adjustment is reached. One sees that the entire argument here is completely consistent with that which we presented earlier in discussing the example of a sole factor of production.

The mechanism of the law of costs must bring about two equivalencies:

1. The equality of the price of each factor of production with the price of the marginal product of this factor of production; and

2. The equality of the price of all cost-expenditures (including the entrepreneur's profit) with the total revenue.

Thus, the solution to the question of the relationship between factor prices and product prices, which is of decisive importance regarding the employment of different factors of production and which arises whenever there is a multitude of different factors, has been reached.[26]

5. Capital Interest and the Temporal Regulation of the Structure of Production

We have already pointed out that as a rule, it is possible to expand production by means of two methods: On the one hand, by increasing the factors of production employed where this increased employment will be subject to the law of diminishing returns; and, on the other hand, by expanding production without increasing the number of factors of production such that a temporal pushing back of the initial employment of individual factors of production takes place and the result of this choice of lengthier roundabout methods of production is an increase in output. We discussed this in great detail in connection with the

---

[26]On the question of the "coordination" of both previously mentioned equalities, see the explanation of Philip Wicksteed and John Hicks.

doctrine of the roundabout methods of production. There it was also explained that the possibilities of lengthening the roundabout methods of production—inasmuch as such a thing may be desirable because of its higher productivity—are limited because the length of the possible roundabout method of production is constrained by the supply of capital. It is now our task to integrate the doctrine of the roundabout method of production with the theory of the formation of prices of factors of production and the law of costs. In an economy that is characterized by exchanges and in which the individual owners of factors of production can measure the success or lack of success of their economic activity in terms of prices, the employment of capital—the choice of a roundabout method of production—can only be directed by the formation of prices. The owner of capital will measure in terms of prices how he can correctly, i.e., with the greatest possible revenue for him, invest his capital. The first question now is which prices are significant here.

Let us assume an entrepreneur chooses to organize a roundabout production process. In order to clearly see the function of capital here, let us assume there is an entrepreneur without any assets who obtains capital from an owner of capital. We will assume further—in order not to complicate matters unnecessarily—that the entrepreneur only needs laborers in addition to the capital he has acquired.

If availability of capital means nothing other than the possibility of beginning roundabout methods of production, thus using factors of production today which only later provide a return, then this capital market is essentially characterized by an exchange of "present goods" for "future goods." The owner of capital gives the entrepreneur something making it possible for the entrepreneur to "invest" what he has received in a roundabout method of production, whereby the owner of capital is satisfied with a return that can only be made when the roundabout method of production has been successfully completed. And if we now ask what the owner of capital hands over to the entrepreneur, then in a first step (and recalling here our previously discussed most elementary case) we can identify this capital with a subsistence fund. Here we are faced with a case of organizing a production process employing capital out of the "state of nature" in which an economy does not yet possess any produced factors of production. The only form of capital present is saved means of subsistence. The entrepreneur will no longer employ his hired laborers in "momentary production"—this, of course, would be the opposite of choosing a roundabout method of production—and pay their wages out of the immediate return from this production process, but instead he will direct labor into the roundabout method of production until the products are achieved, and will pay the laborers out of the free capital that he has acquired from the owner of capital. The subsistence fund, which alone assumes the function of capital, serves to support the laborers for the duration of the roundabout production process and thereby is used up successively. It is clear that the entrepreneur cannot employ laborers—who themselves are not owners of capital and who thus must continuously reap a return for their labor in a roundabout production process—unless he has access to a subsistence fund.

Now, in order to obtain supply and demand curves, let us assume that in an economy which heretofore has worked exclusively in momentary production, a number of entrepreneurs in one or a few lines of production in which the choice of roundabout production methods can bring about a large increase in returns begin to introduce roundabout production methods by employing subsistence funds in the way just described. It is possible for them to do this because other economic subjects who have become owners of capital by saving have offered them a subsistence fund for future returns on the emerging capital market. If entrepreneurs attract laborers from other production processes—we have assumed that labor is the sole factor of production for simplicity's sake—and begin roundabout methods of production, then in the end they will attain a larger return with these laborers than would have been possible in momentary production. If we wish to follow this process in the realm of prices, we will notice two movements: First, the laborers' wages will have risen. For the laborers will only be drawn out of their previous employment with higher wages. However, this change might not be very significant if introducing a roundabout method of production only affects a relatively small part of the economy. It can even be completely absent if we imagine that entrepreneurs who until now have worked in momentary production begin to introduce roundabout production methods with the previously employed laborers. Second, however—and this is of greater significance—we will have to expect a drop in the price of the product after the completion of the roundabout method of production. This is because in roundabout production more products can be produced. Because of this movement in prices, the span which the greater productivity of the roundabout method of production leaves open for profit above labor costs will be reduced. We will now see that with a correct entrepreneurial decision, however, some such span must nonetheless remain, and hence, a roundabout method of production can only be adopted if such a span between the costs of labor and the price of the product exists.

In order to illustrate this clearly we would like to use a formulation which was used previously. The entrepreneur has two possibilities for expanding production: He can either employ more laborers, or lengthen the roundabout production process. With respect to employing more laborers the situation is obvious; in this case a linear expansion of production takes place. In the same momentary production, twice as many laborers will produce twice as many products.[27] With respect to lengthening the roundabout method of production, however, something must be added to what we have already said about this situation.

It cannot be doubted that a "cleverly chosen" extension of the roundabout method of production, i.e., the introduction of a time span between the expenditure of the factor of production and the attainment of the finished product, can increase returns. Once this point of departure is secured, that which makes the roundabout method of production possible must be regarded as a means of increasing output, just as would an additional amount of any originary means of production. We can label "that which makes the roundabout method of production possible" a factor of production P_1, just as we call labor or land factors of production. P_1 can be "combined" with another factor of production P_2—for example, human labor—whereby extensive variability in the way in which they can be combined exists. The interaction of two economic

---

[27]A decreasing output cannot be considered because we have assumed that labor is the sole factor of production.

factors of production, however, must be subject to the principle of diminishing returns.[28] This means that the combination of a given quantity of P_1 with an increasing number of units of P_2 will result in an always decreasing growth in output. We first presented the deduction of this principle of the interaction of factors of production with respect to the so-called law of diminishing returns of agricultural production, and we then immediately recognized that it is a general principle of the combination of factors of production: No one would offer anything for the addition of P_1 in production if it were possible, solely by means of increasing the use of P_2, to attain a proportionally increased output. From this it follows that if any combination of P_1 and P_2 is given, a "decreasing" increased output can be achieved by adding individual units of P_1, or by adding individual units of P_2. Hence, the law of marginal productivity is applicable for P_1 as well as for P_2. It is thereby irrelevant which kind of production factor it is, whether it is labor or land or "that which makes the adoption of roundabout methods of production possible." We have now arrived at the application of the principle of marginal productivity regarding the employment of capital. Since the use of free capital in our examples has permitted the choice of the roundabout method of production, and since the "factor of production" which by lengthening the roundabout method of production permits the increase in output is the subsistence fund, this factor also receives a share of the returns according to its marginal product.

Recall again our earlier formulation. The entrepreneur takes on the consumers' demand and transforms it into a demand for various factors of production. He will be able to pay for each factor of production according to its marginal productivity. In so doing, he will prefer that factor of production which provides him with a greater return at a lower cost, and he will get rid of individual units of those factors of production whose marginal product is less than the price he would have to pay to use it until the marginal product is equal to this price. He will not use a single unit of a factor of production that does not at least result in a growth in output equivalent to the cost of using this factor. This holds for labor and land, as well as for the subsistence fund. In "correctly" carrying out production, the entrepreneur can return

---

[28]Compare here the explanations on pp. 85ff.

not only this subsistence fund to those who provide him with it, thereby making the introduction of a roundabout method of production possible, but in addition he can also pay them interest. The former is obvious, for the size of the subsistence fund that is used in production is identical to the sum of wages. This cost expenditure must be covered by the product. But the latter is also clear, for each "ration" of the subsistence fund which has served to pay a wage has meant not only that a labor unit could be employed, but also that it could be employed earlier in production to the same extent as the length of time for which this subsistence fund had been tied up in the production process. If it had not been for this portion of the subsistence fund, the labor could still have been employed—but only at the last moment in production when it would have received wages directly from returns. The fact that this labor could be employed earlier, thus increasing returns, is the result of the cooperation of the subsistence fund. Increased output is solely the result of this circumstance—increased returns are dependent on the condition that a subsistence fund is used. Thus the employment of a subsistence fund must create a time span between the costs of labor and the price of the product. A part of the returns, which can be described in terms of marginal productivity, is dependent on the expenditure of a subsistence fund. For this reason, an entrepreneur can pay interest according to the marginal product.[29] However, the entrepreneur will also have to pay capital interest as long as a limited supply of capital is faced with a demand which can increase its output by using more capital, by lengthening the roundabout method of production. Only if the entrepreneur can pay capital interest will he be able to keep pace with entrepreneurs competing with him on the capital market.

We noted earlier that the higher returns to be expected from the adoption of roundabout methods of production will bring about a tendency to reduce the profit margin by causing, on the one hand, wages to rise, and on the other hand, product prices to fall. Now it may be briefly mentioned that the situation of

---

[29]Knut Wicksell formulates this as follows: "Capital is saved labor and saved soil energies; capital interest is the difference between the marginal productivity of saved (stored up) labor and soil energies and the marginal productivity of current (present) ones." (*Lectures*, vol. 1, p. 154.)

choosing roundabout methods of production is no different from that of introducing any new production process. When any new production process is begun, the entrepreneur must attract factors of production, and in increasing the products, he will push down their prices. However, in the case of a "correct choice," he will only begin such production processes which, in spite of these counter effects, do not lead to any losses. Obviously, the appearance of one single entrepreneur will often neither drive up the price of a factor of production so dramatically nor force the price of the product down so far that it would be necessary to be concerned about these two movements. Here we only point out this case in order to be able to apply it to the case of introducing roundabout methods of production: Here, too, the entrepreneur will only be able to adopt roundabout methods of production that yield a surplus return and thus allow him to pay capital interest in addition to his other costs.

The rest is simply the application of a line of reasoning with which we are already familiar. For a moment, let us further consider the subsistence fund as a form of capital. The more capital of this kind that is formed, the more and the longer roundabout methods of production can be introduced until in the end all production is carried out using roundabout methods. The greater productivity of these roundabout methods of production will actually vary. Those roundabout methods of production which result in the greatest capital return will be preferred. The changes will thereby not only be restricted to changes from one production process to another, not only to an expansion of one and a reduction of another production, but also within the individual production processes the roundabout methods will have to be shortened or lengthened. It is not the subsistence fund as such that is traded on the capital market, but capital that is free for some time until it is repaid, i.e., something which can be captured by the formula: capital multiplied by time. And finally, it is clear that in a smoothly operating model, a price in the form of a uniform interest rate must arise for this object on the capital market. The owners of capital will try to achieve the highest possible interest rate; and as a result of the greater productivity of the roundabout methods of production, the entrepreneurs will be in a position to pay back what they have received plus interest. The supply of the owners of capital is faced with the entrepreneurs' demand which will be stratified according to the degree of greater productivity of the individual roundabout method of production and its suitability for supporting a higher or lower interest rate. Just as with each price formation, that demand will succeed which is capable of paying the highest price, in this case the highest interest rate. Among all of the possible roundabout methods of production, only those will be able to be carried out which can produce surplus returns that are in line with the market rate of interest. Those roundabout production processes that cannot pay this free-market interest rate must not be started. However, the stratification of the demand for capital is not only determined by the possibility of achieving a larger or smaller return in one or another line of production, but beyond this is determined by the possibility of achieving a larger or smaller increase in returns, depending on the duration of each individual production process. Consequently, we see the decisive function of capital interest: it alone offers the possibility to the entrepreneur of determining time limits for the roundabout method of production. Lowering the interest rate offers the possibility of investing capital in even more lengthy roundabout methods of production, i.e., in those in which the "marginal product" of capital is lower, while a rise in the interest rate forces a shortening of the roundabout method of production.

It is exclusively the height of interest—and not, for example, the size of the subsistence fund that he plans to use as capital—that has become a new cost factor for the entrepreneur employing capital in a production process. For in the case considered here—of production carried out from beginning to end by one entrepreneur such that no capital goods arrive on the market—capital is identical to the sum of wages that the entrepreneur must "advance" to laborers before the product is completed. The situation is simply that each prior wage expenditure must not only find an equivalent in its product, but this product must also include capital interest as determined by the length of time for which this capital has been "tied up." Any other use of a subsistence fund cannot be justified in the framework of price calculations. In a complex economy, the owner of capital must invest his subsistence fund in such a way that each time his capital is invested, he receives the interest rate prevailing for this time period on the market. The entrepreneur will not be able to obtain capital if he cannot carry this "additional" cost burden.

One must pay attention, however, to the fact that as a result of the above mentioned possible variations in the employment of capital, with respect to capital the "mechanism" of the law of costs will be more complicated than with regard to other production factors. In any case, the principle of the marginal product will be applicable here, too. More capital means an increase in a production factor which will be subject to the law of diminishing returns. Let it only be said here that the "clever choice" of productive combinations will prefer that kind of rearrangement between production factors for which the expected surplus return is greater. The same will also apply to the case of restricting the employment of capital in production.

It will not be difficult for us to proceed now from the construed case of carrying out production by one entrepreneur from beginning to end to that corresponding to a real economy in which production is not carried out without interruption by one single entrepreneur, but instead is distributed "vertically" among a number of entrepreneurs. What emerges as a problem in this case is the formation of the prices of capital goods. Since it is obvious that the prices of these capital goods as well as all other prices of products in the course of a static economy will be cost prices, it suffices here to give a brief indication of the effect of cost expenditures within continuously proceeding production. In breaking down this production, the capital good will have to be exchanged at that price which corresponds to the costs expended in the course of production. These cost expenditures determine at each moment the cost value of the product which becomes the cost price and hence, with an organization of production corresponding to the law of costs, determine the market price as soon as the capital good leaves the firm and arrives on the market. It should now be beyond any doubt that for each previously expended unit of capital, interest is calculated according to the length of time the capital was tied up, and must be included in the costs. Similarly, it cannot be doubted that interest will also have to be calculated as a cost factor of the capital good according to the period of time for which capital is tied up.

Finally, it is also clear that wherever a capital good (a machine) is used to produce a greater number of product units which can only be completed over a longer period of time, the average duration of the tying up of capital invested in this factor of production must be included in the calculation of the cost burden of interest. The principle of price formation for durable capital goods will thus take effect in the same way as for intermediate products.

If, however, capital interest becomes the selection principle for choosing the length of the roundabout method of production, then it will also determine the extent to which free capital can be transformed into durable capital goods. Durable goods only come about through the investment of free capital, just as do intermediate products. The entrepreneur who produces durable capital goods chooses a particularly long roundabout method of production; he invests free capital in a roundabout method of production from which only later can a complete release be possible. Hence, it is clear that a lower interest rate will encourage the formation of durable capital goods. From this it is obvious how necessary the calculation of interest is for roundabout production. Without a calculation of interest there would be absolutely no indication to what extent the tying up of capital in durable investments is possible without a lack of the complementary good of free capital arising. More will have to be said about this relationship later.

6. The Supply of Capital

Earlier we pointed out that new capital can only emerge in the form of free capital. The means of subsistence which an economic subject receives as income will not be consumed, but instead will be supplied for a roundabout method of production. The sole source of any new capital in a market economy[30] is a change in the use of income, such that one who earns income and could otherwise consume it makes the means of subsistence available in order to initiate a roundabout production process. We can picture these provisions for a roundabout method of production

---

[30]Neither here nor in the following are we interested in the problem of the qualitative composition of free capital.

such that this subsistence fund is given to an entrepreneur who with its help begins a roundabout method of production and only later pays back his debts out of the returns from production. The entrepreneur purchases factors of production with the free capital—let us assume first he pays laborers. The free capital will now be consumed by the laborers, and the entrepreneur possesses those capital goods—transformed raw materials or durable investments—that the laborers have produced. Once the production process is completed, the originally expended free capital is reproduced (plus interest; but that is not important here), and it can be returned to the owner of capital. This reproduction occurs more or less quickly, depending on how the free capital is used. Insofar as free capital is employed in a consumption related stage of production for the payment of laborers, it becomes freely available at the completion of production, and free capital in the form of new consumer goods is regenerated. If capital is used in earlier stages of production, then its release takes longer because the consumer goods in whose production the capital played a role only become available at the completion of the entire production process. If, however, the capital is invested in the production of fixed capital, then the waiting time until it can be regenerated is significantly lengthened: it will only be successively released when consumer goods with this investment are completed to the extent that a renewal fund is created during continuous production. Thus, the length of time free capital is tied up in the production process will vary greatly. Yet each portion of the free capital that is employed in the production process, even that which is used in the "heaviest" investments, must in the end be transformed into the originary form of capital, into free capital. The owner of the capital can again put this free capital to the same use: It remains available to the entrepreneur who repeats the same production process. In this case, the once-formed capital is maintained; it changes again more or less slowly from the form of capital goods into the form of consumer goods which are then reinvested. A loss will only occur where production was unsuccessful. This can mean that production failed in a technical sense; in economic fluctuations, however, it can also happen that a technically successful production process fails because it is not integrated into the framework of the economy and does not find a corresponding demand willing to pay. There will be more to say on this later. There is, however, something more to be said on the question of the liquidity of capital investments.

The principle that free capital once integrated into the production process only becomes available again when its products are completed—and under certain circumstances this can mean a long time—is perfectly compatible with the fact that in a market economy much higher private liquidity exists. This follows from each vertical differentiation of production. When an entrepreneur produces a capital good and sells this to an entrepreneur who needs it—perhaps as a renewal for his investment while he receives free capital in return—the free capital invested in this capital good becomes available again to the entrepreneur who produced it; in particular he can pay the borrowed capital back to the owner. It should be clear that the capital actually invested here will not become free in this exchange, but that two capital owners here merely switch their positions: the buyer who had free capital transfers it to an entrepreneur in exchange for capital tied up in capital goods. The proportion of free capital to capital goods (tied up capital) in an economy cannot be altered by such an exchange.

We have already dealt with the question of the price of capital goods under the assumption of an effectively operating law of costs. Each capital good represents a specific stage in the process of employing factors of production for the production of consumer goods. And just as according to the law of costs the price of the expenditures must be equal to the price of the product, so must at each stage of the production process the price of a capital good be equal to the sum of the expenditures necessary for its production, or the discounted price of the product minus the expenditures still necessary for its completion. Supply and demand will respond to every deviation in the price of a capital good from this height; movements will then be set in motion with the tendency towards adjusting to the cost price. It is obvious that here the reactions of the supply will often only become effective relatively late because the creation of many products requires a lengthy production time. During fluctuations in the economy, the fact that capital is tied up in lengthy roundabout methods of production can result in significant gains and losses in capital goods. In the first case, incomes will be produced which could bring about an expansion in the formation of capital through savings, and in the second case it can happen that the necessary renewal fund is not formed and thus capital is consumed. Regarding the formation of the price of capital goods, however, the principle applying to all products will in any case hold: it is not the size of the expenditures that determines the price, but the demanding entrepreneur's willingness and ability to pay. If a large revenue can be expected for a product, the price of the capital good will reflect this; if a smaller revenue is expected, the price will fall without regard to the costs incurred. Only changes in the supply of a capital good will bring about an adjustment of these prices toward actual costs.

The available supply of capital in an economy, the available free capital and the existing capital goods are in constant motion during continuous production. Free capital becomes tied up and new free capital grows continually out of capital goods. Clearly the owner of capital is subject to more fluctuations in the course of the economy than the owner of other factors of production—of laborers as well as land. Losses which occur if production does not lead to success will only too quickly reduce the extent to which free capital is formed; large profits will make the further formation of new capital possible. Movements which occur in the various lines of production for different firms determine, in the sum of their effects, the amount of free capital available, and hence the possibility of adopting roundabout methods of production; and they thereby determine the size of the success of production in an economy in which production occurs exclusively in roundabout ways.

One more thing should be said here. Much energy has been spent attempting to present the formation of new capital in the form of a supply curve. Since what the saver receives as compensation for refraining from consumption and providing the capital—as a wage[31] for the "act of saving"—is capital interest, a question must be raised regarding the relationship between the

---

[31]Clearly, this expression is subject to misinterpretation as expressing a value-judgment ("just" wage). The more correct formulation would be: "economic successor of consumption sacrifices."

amount of savings and the height of capital interest. One must note that the argument to be applied in this case will hardly lead to a clear-cut result. It is probably justified to say that a higher interest rate will stimulate savings, and that consequently the supply of newly formed capital grows at a higher interest rate and that there will also be an increased incentive to maintain and avoid capital consumption, while on the other hand a lower interest rate will lead to a reduction in savings and—what is perhaps still more important—reduces the inhibitions which keep some individuals from consuming capital. One could then come to the conclusion that a drop in the interest rate below a certain minimum will not be possible because the lack of new formation of capital and the increased consumption of capital would so drastically reduce the supply of capital that the interest rate would in turn have to rise. Without disputing that these connections generally exist, we must point out here, however, that the opposite relationship can also exist: Whoever saves in order to achieve a certain income from interest will achieve this income earlier with higher interest and hence will cease to save sooner. Since one must undoubtedly consider this relationship as possible, it follows that a general proposition regarding a necessary relationship between savings and capital interest is not at all possible.

7. The Prices of Original Factors of Production in Capitalist Production

The theoretical determination of the wage rate on the free market follows without difficulty from the application of the general law of prices and the principle of marginal productivity. The price will form at the level at which the supply of laborers is equal to the entrepreneurs' demand. Since an entrepreneur must shape his demand according to the size of the marginal product—he cannot offer more or he would suffer a loss in hiring labor, he also will not be able to hire the laborer more cheaply since he would be able to find employment elsewhere at a wage equal to the size of the marginal product—the price of labor will coincide with the price of the marginal product. If one considers the supply of laborers as stratified according to its urgency, then the wage will be equivalent to the supply of the "most expensive" (that is, the one coming onto the market with the highest supply) of those laborers who are still employed.[32] Thus, we have determined the principle according to which the laborers' share in the product. In the case of momentary production this suffices. However, when considering a time consuming roundabout structure of production a complication results, because the size of the wage sum is also determined by the amount of wage capital or that portion of free capital which is available for the payment of wages.

This is easy to see. Ignore the cooperating effect of the second originary factor of production of land and that part of human labor which is occupied exclusively with the immediate completion of consumer goods, so that the product can be completed without the laborer having to be paid a wage in advance.[33] It is clear that all other laborers produce something that can only be enjoyed much later as a consumer good. The laborers must have some means of support while the fruits of their labor are developing into a consumer good. The necessary subsistence fund must be made available lest roundabout production be impossible.[34] The function of whoever makes this fund available is that of the owner of capital; the one who makes present goods available in order to receive them back later.

---

[32]One is reminded here of the famous formulation of Thünen. If we interpret the quantity **a** in the sense of marginal analysis as the representation of the smallest wage (support) for which those of the employed laborers who are subject to the lowest social pressure are still willing to work, and if—again in line with marginal analysis—we interpret the quantity **p** as the product of the "last" laborer still employed (marginal product of labor), then **a** is equal to **p** and the height of the wage is determined by each of these quantities or also by the formula

$$\sqrt{a \cdot p}$$

[33]This is to say, ignoring that labor for which no "economically relevant" time-period passes between its employment and the attainment of a finished consumer good (see on this note 3). It should be clear that consideration of production then only excludes a relatively small sector of labor services from analysis.

[34]If the laborer himself possesses this subsistence fund, then in this respect he himself is, of course, a "capitalist." The theoretical analysis must, however, set out from a consideration in which the various functions are differentiated, as only then will the function of each factor of production—and in roundabout production one of these is free capital—for structuring production be recognized correctly.

This would also be valid if the "union of personality" between laborer and owner of the capital were of greater significance in practice than is actually the case today.

It is important here to keep in mind the integration of this process of investing capital in the course of the entire economy. The entrepreneur who pays laborers a wage in production processes that precede the production of consumer goods immediately receives a return value in the form of a finished article whose value is increased through processing and—with a vertical structuring of production in individual firms—can be sold on the market. Upon sale of the capital good, the entrepreneur immediately receives something of equivalent value in return. An "advance" for labor appears to be necessary primarily for the time between the payment to the laborer and the sale of the product; in no case, however, is this necessary for the time between the payment for labor and the creation of a consumer good produced by means of a capital good—which can often only be expected after a great length of time. So this situation appears in the entrepreneur's calculation: his free capital must make production possible from the introduction of labor until the sale of his product. He is not further interested in whether what he has produced is a finished consumer good or a capital good that will perhaps only result in a consumer good after a long period of time. In particular, the real goods perspective shows that a subsistence fund functioning as capital is the prerequisite for the adoption of a time-consuming roundabout method of production. Payment for the result of preceding production processes can only occur in the form of means of subsistence; and this is so because an entrepreneur carrying out preceding production processes can support those who produce a product that is not yet ready for consumption only by using means of subsistence. If a subsistence fund is employed in this way, it means that it is invested in production, that it is only employed to produce finished consumer goods at a later time. Capital invested in this way will only become available again when at the completion of the production process it is freed up. During this entire time it remains tied up and this time between investment and release must be bridged. We have already seen that synchronization does not change anything concerning this relationship.[35]

---

[35]One thing must be repeated here: It is not necessary for a capitalist whose capital is invested, for example, in a roundabout method of production lasting

Insofar, then, as labor is used in the roundabout method of production, its expenditure is dependent on the provision of a subsistence fund. We have already said that it would be a mistake to simply label the finished consumer goods available in the economy—and in considering a time period in which several synchronized production processes are completed, also the consumer goods maturing during this time—as a fund available for the support of laborers. These consumer goods are only capital insofar as their owners employ them in the function of capital, and as they are employed for the purpose of investment. We earlier used the phrase: for "reproductive consumption."

If the payment for laborers employed in the roundabout method of production can only come from a subsistence fund functioning as capital, then from this follows a determination of the size of the wages. When we said that the laborers' share in the product is determined by the size of the marginal product of labor, we stated that—in a certain sense—productivity of labor is the basis for determining the height of wages. We now see a very different determining cause for the labor wage: *No more of the means of subsistence can be transferred over to laborers employed in a roundabout method of production than have been saved by the owners of capital and made available for the purpose of investing.* The size of the

---

two years, to actually wait two years for his capital to be freed up. He can sell the produced capital good and receive in return free capital. However, the sale of a pre-product is, of course, only possible if another capitalist can spare free capital in payment and—taking the first capitalist's place, so to speak—keep his capital tied up until production is completed or until a new sale is made. If invested capital becomes free in this way before production is completed, then from the point of view which looks beyond the situation of the individual, this is nothing but an "interpersonal change in the position of liquidity." That such a change recurs, in particular with synchronized production processes—namely every time a capital good moves on from one stage of production to the next carried out by a different entrepreneur—must not distract from the fact that even in synchronized production the payment for a capital good with free capital is only possible because earlier, in another process of production, consumer goods already had been created that assumed the function of free capital. Not recognizing that the synchronization cannot change the essence of roundabout production and that with synchronized production, too, the implementation of roundabout methods of production is only possible if "free capital" has been made available, has led repeatedly to grave errors.

sum of wages is hence identical to the size of the saved and invested share of the output of consumer goods.[36]

The important question now is how what we have learned about the wage fund is compatible with what we have learned about the significance of marginal productivity in determining the wage height. An answer to this question can be found without difficulty if one makes the effort to draw the final consequences from the principle which gives rise to the problem of the wage fund. We must assume that we are speaking of a production process during which an "economically relevant" period of time passes between the employment of labor and the achievement of the finished product of consumer goods—a time period during which the support of the laborers requires provision. Furthermore, we must consider that within capitalist production a more or less wide expansion of roundabout methods of production is possible and that such an expansion would be in the interest of increasing returns, but that it finds its limits in the availability of support. The wage fund always serves to provide for the laborers during a specific time period. If in dividing the wage fund we consider as a variable the time for which it must prove sufficient, then the connection between the law of marginal productivity and the division of a wage fund becomes apparent.

The wage fund must be sufficient to pay the laborers' wages for the duration of the roundabout method of production. If it is not sufficient for this, then this is an indication that too lengthy roundabout production processes have been chosen. The insufficient supply of free capital must drive up the interest rate and thereby force a shortening of the roundabout production processes. Since a shortened roundabout production process is equivalent to a lower marginal product of labor, wages must fall. Simultaneously, the number of employed will go down (with a corresponding shape of the labor supply). Thus, we see that with an insufficient supply of wage funds the length of the roundabout production process goes down, wages drop and the number of

---

[36]The wage fund is thereby not only that part of the output of consumer goods which is newly saved, but also that part which was saved earlier and is now maintained.

laborers will become smaller. An adjustment of demand to the size of the wage fund is thereby brought about. One must keep in mind that this adjustment is required by the interest rate. We see the reverse case when the wage fund is greater than the demand arising from the given production structure. A lowering of the interest rate will lead to a lengthening of the roundabout production process, to a rise in wages and under certain circumstances to an increase in the number of employed persons. In both cases, a structure of production results in which the wage fund suffices to pay all employed persons according to the size of the marginal product of labor for the duration of the roundabout method of production.[37]

In the framework of the doctrine of the roundabout methods of production, attention must be paid to two important principles regarding the relationships between wage and capital. On the one hand, there is the principle of the complementarity of labor and wage fund, i.e., the rule that labor can only be employed in a roundabout production process if a wage fund is available as a complementary good. On the other hand, there is

---

[37]In my article mentioned on page 165, Number 1, I have presented these relationships in a formula. If **W** is the size of the wage fund, **l** the number of laborers, **r** the quantity of rations into which the wage fund is divided, **p** the number of payments which occur during the roundabout method of production (for example, wage weeks), and finally, **m** the size of the marginal product, the following equations can be formulated:

$$W = l \cdot r \cdot p$$
$$r = m$$

If the wage fund is not equal to the quantity on the right side of the wage fund equation, all three quantities which are on this side change as a result of changes in the interest rate. If **W** is smaller, a rise in the interest rate will reduce the magnitude **p** (by shortening the duration of the roundabout production process), **r**, and perhaps also **l**, until equality is reached. In contrast, a larger **W** will lead to a lower interest rate and increase the magnitude on the right side of the equation.

In this essay I have indicated a second possible tendency towards equalization: If the magnitude **W** is too small and the interest rate rises, then it can happen that greater saving increases the supply of free capital.

In this case, a fall in the magnitudes on the right side of the equation will contrast with a rise in the magnitude **W**, so that the equalization will be facilitated. The reverse can occur if the interest rate falls.

the principle that the virulence of capital—its ability to make more or less lengthy roundabout production processes possible—is dependent on the wage rate. There is still more to be said here regarding these two statements.

Labor can also be employed other than in a roundabout method of production. If a laborer picks berries, no expenditure of capital is necessary—the laborer will live off the daily output of his labor or, respectively, from its revenue. In this way only a limited number of laborers will earn a very minimal living. Further, it will be difficult to find many other examples of this kind today which shows how far removed we presently are from the conditions of momentary production. The use of a subsistence fund as a complementary good to labor is furthermore not necessary where we are concerned with the last stage of a roundabout method of production in which the duration of production is so short that an "advance" for labor is not necessary. We have already presented the example of a baker. Let us make only one more point in this connection. The more plentiful the supply of capital in an economy, the more significance labor will lose in the last stage of production as compared to labor employed in preceding production stages. In a modern bread factory, the number of laborers directly producing the bread will be significantly lower in relation to the total output than under conditions of primitive hand work. In the first case, a greater amount of capital made the adoption of a longer roundabout production process possible, and the essence of lengthening the roundabout method of production is that in the course of the entire production process the expenditure of labor is moved back in time into production processes that precede those of consumer goods production. It has already been explained in detail that in the process of lengthening the roundabout method of production, the formation of durable capital investments is only one particularly important occurrence. However, the more that labor is shifted into earlier stages in the course of production, the greater will be that sector of labor which can only be employed by drawing on a complementary wage fund.

Now, for the length of possible roundabout production processes it is not only the size of the wage fund as such that is decisive, but also the size of the rations distributed to the laborers. The smaller the ration, the larger will be the productive power of the wage fund, the longer will be the roundabout production processes which can be begun, and the larger will also be the return of production. Hence, temporarily low wages would be in the interest of an increase in production which in turn would make higher wages possible. This, however, is so *given the essential condition* that the greater output of production serves to expand the supply of capital, i.e., that there are savings. With the formation of wage prices, as theoretically follows from the interaction of supply and demand under the condition of a free, competitive market, the level of wages and thus the productive power of available capital is determined clearly. The laborer cannot receive less than his marginal product. Regulating the length of the roundabout method of production by means of the interest rate will cause the wage fund to suffice as the wage sum. It can be of interest here, however, if we consider the case in which the conditions of the labor market are such that not all laborers who are prepared to work can also be employed. The problem of unemployment caused by friction in the market does not interest us here. We will not speak of unemployment in a technical sense if all laborers willing to work for the going wage prices find work, and if in addition there are still laborers who do not find employment because they are only prepared to work for higher wages.

There are two cases, however, in which it is possible that at a given wage price the supply of laborers is greater than the demand for them. First, the wage price is fixed above the free-market price by wage decrees from outside the market economy. And second, the supply of laborers is such that at the wages formed on the free market a greater number of laborers are willing to work than the demand can assume.[38] Let us initially consider the first of these two cases.

---

[38]In the first case, the price on the free market would be **OA**. At this price the supply would be equal to the demand (**OM**). The price tax of the height **OB** causes the demand to fall to **OM'**, while at this wage the supply of laborers is equal to **OM"**. In the second case, the wage on the free market would be determined by the intersection point of the supply and demand curve, but at this price there would be a supply **OM'** as opposed to a demand **OM**, because the supply curve for labor to the right of the point of intersection moves horizontally.

The labor supply **MM'** cannot find employment at this wage because at this wage level the supply is greater than demand. In spite of this discrepancy between supply and demand, this supply cannot function to reduce wages because it is only willing to work for the wage price **OA**. Without a doubt, both of

When wages are artificially maintained, the process of adjusting the number of laborers, the wage height, and the length, of the roundabout production processes (which we mentioned when presenting the wage fund equation) cannot take its course unhampered, because the wage height is a fixed quantity. Clearly, the rigidity of this magnitude must result in even stronger movements in the other two magnitudes. Under otherwise equal conditions, a rise in wages would reduce the number of laborers and shorten the length of the roundabout production process. The movement of these two magnitudes could adjust the product of the three magnitudes on the right side of the wage fund equation to the size of the wage fund even if the wage rate remains rigid.

One must, however, be aware of one point here. Maintaining a wage at this height has the result that firms can only employ laborers insofar as the marginal product of labor is raised. If we ignore entirely the possibility of varying the length of the roundabout production process, this can only occur if there are "more favorable" production possibilities, while one would have to abstain from less favorable ones. Thus, the direction of the adjustment will be towards limiting production which for technical reasons (such as an unfavorable location) is more expensive. Furthermore, there will be an adjustment towards abstaining from all production processes which can only achieve

---

these cases of unemployment are possible. The question which of these two cases is more important in practice is a question of applying this scheme to reality, not a question of theory. Let it only be said here that the second case in particular will occur if in one country the productivity for some reason—for example, the disintegration from a more comprehensive system of interlocal division of labor or a relevant decrease in the supply of capital—has been reduced significantly. "Cyclical" unemployment will require special consideration later on.

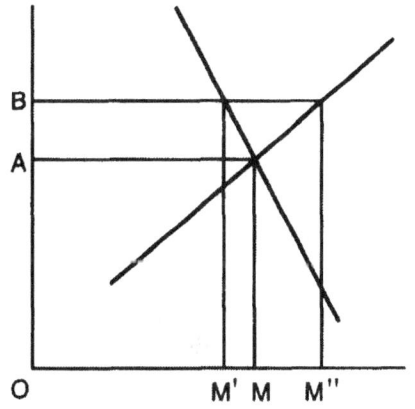 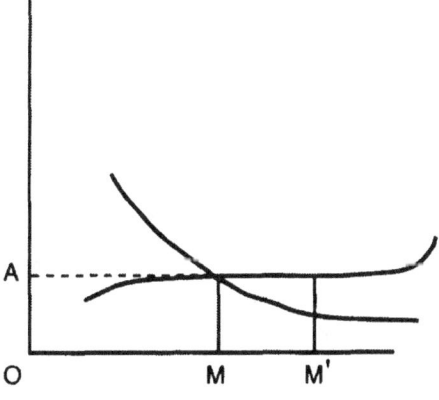

a lower revenue for their product. Hence, the movement tends in the direction of eliminating the least productive laborers with the goal of raising the marginal product. In addition, a tendency towards shortening the length of the roundabout production processes, which leads to a reduction in the size of the marginal product, would work against the first tendency. Clearly, this conflict can only be solved such that a tendency towards reducing the number of laborers is markedly more effective than the tendency towards shortening the roundabout methods of production. For it is obvious that the more the number of employees drops, the less likely will the increase in rations into which the wage fund is divided cause a shortening of the roundabout method of production.

In the second instance of unemployment of which we have spoken, the wage is a free-market price, although the supply of laborers is larger than the demand. This case is nonetheless analogous to the first case insofar as the height of wages is rigid; however, this is only so because of the particular form of the supply. Adjusting the number of employed to the length of the roundabout method of production does not cause further theoretical difficulties in this case.

Here one must briefly point out how these instances of unemployment must be classified in the historical process of economic development. An "artificial" wage increase will lead to problems of adjustment which under all circumstances will probably lead to the consumption of capital. This is so because the amount of capital already invested, i.e., the supply of capital goods—in particular of fixed capital—must be adjusted to new conditions. Practically speaking, this means that the capital invested cannot be freed up entirely without losses. Ignoring this transitional time period, too high a wage must be incorporated into the course of a static economic system.[39] Naturally, the consequence

---

[39]Here the problem for economic theory is essentially no different than in the case in which a corresponding number of laborers is reduced—for example, by emigration. In the static system, a rise in wages is equivalent to a reduction in the number of laborers. Note in addition, that insofar as the unemployed are maintained "at the cost of the economy," i.e., insofar as subsidies for the maintenance of the unemployed become production costs (the maintenance of the unemployed does not come out of other income), here, too, the incorporation of the situation into the static system is possible, although the rise in costs must again imply a restriction in production possibilities.

of this will be the nonemployment of laborers. Doing away with unemployment will only be possible in two ways: Either the economic conditions will change in the direction of making production possibilities more favorable,[40] or, and this is the only other possibility to eliminate unemployment, the level of wages will be reduced. Assuming that before, wages have been artificially raised, this can only happen if wage determination that takes place outside the free market adjusts to free-market pricing. However, where the structure of the supply of labor also leads to unemployment on the free market, a reduction in wages will only occur when increased social pressure brought about by persistent unemployment leads to a change in the structure of the supply of labor, to a reduction in the "aspirations" of the laborers.

In addition to labor, the second originary factor of production must be discussed. We have always equated the performance of land and soil with that of labor. Hence, we assume here that we have an originary factor of production whose cooperation in production brings about an output only later, while the payment for this achievement must be made today. The free capital, or the subsistence fund which functions as free capital, is not merely the fund out of which wages are paid, but the fund out of which wages and annuities are paid. Let us try to justify this view.

The need to find special justification results from the fact that the advance for the owner of land—his payment *before* the finished product is produced—is not necessary in the same sense as the advanced payment for labor. The laborer cannot work and under certain circumstances must wait years for his wages, whereas the productivity of land in no way becomes worse, even if the owner of the soil himself dies of starvation. Consider the following scenario: The owner of land makes his soil available for production and only later receives his (soil's) share of the product, while in the meantime he lives from other means—perhaps as a laborer or an owner of capital. Clearly, however, this is a combination of different functions within one person, and in order to present the formations of supply and demand in a pure form, we have always assumed a complete personal separation of

---

[40]To continue with the previously introduced examples: Measures which have restricted the division of labor are eliminated; the supply of capital rises, but the chance of this occurring in this connection is probably not very great.

these functions. However, if we consider the owner of land as an economic subject who exclusively controls the production factor of land, then the following picture results: The owner of land sells the productive contribution of his soil on the market in successive steps, just as the laborer his labor. The finished product as an "economic successor" of the productive achievement of land only comes about later, just as is the case regarding labor. And finally, it is without a doubt, that, as is the case with respect to labor, the prior expenditure of land leads to an increase in output. Thus, the contributions of land and soil are fully integrated, in the same way as are those of labor, into the analysis of the roundabout method of production.

This has nothing to do with the social organization of an economy, especially with the existence of private property of land. For here it is no matter of concern who can consume an output, but only how a factor of production is employed in roundabout production. If the state were the owner of all land, it could turn over the return from the land to whomever it pleased. A specific use of land and soil would not depend on a corresponding prior compensation out of free capital; that is, out of the wage and annuities fund. It is also conceivable that that share of free capital which from an economic point of view is an annuities fund will be used to pay laborers employed in roundabout methods of production, either as an additional wage, or in order to lengthen the roundabout methods of production. It is clear how this situation would have to be integrated in our analysis: The state employs the "income" from the land rent, not as remuneration for providing the "productive service" of land, but instead it invests it in an extension of the roundabout method of production. This will not change the fact, however, that land functions as an originary factor of production in roundabout methods of production, and that the way in which it is employed, particularly the earlier or later incorporation of the productive services of land, is a determination of the size of the output.

8. The Principle of Substitution and the Horizontal Connectivity of Prices

If in a smoothly functioning market only one uniform price can arise for goods of the same kind, then it is not much more than a continuation of this thought if this principle is expanded to the law that goods which can be substituted for each other will attain the same price. It is clear that disparities in the prices of goods which can be substituted for each other will lead to changes in the form of supply and demand. This can be most simply explained with respect to the area of consumer goods. If two consumer goods **A** and **B** (for example, foods) can be put to essentially the same use, but good **A** is significantly more expensive than good **B**, then the demand for good **A** will fall whereas the demand for good **B** will rise, thus setting in motion a tendency towards equalizing both prices.[41] This interconnectedness of product prices will also be reflected in a connectivity of prices of factors of production: Since the demand for **A** is co-determined by the price of **B**, the price of a factor of production suitable for product **A** will also be co-determined by the price of the factor of production suitable only for product **B**.

Here we are interested primarily in the interrelation of prices of factors of production resulting from the possibility of substitution. For example, there is the possibility of substituting unskilled for skilled labor. A multitude of unskilled labor can occasionally be substituted for a unit of skilled labor, and this substitution possibility must be reflected in the relation between both prices. Furthermore, there can be a substitution between labor and land: Production by a single entrepreneur can be expanded by increasing labor or by increasing land (and restricted, respectively). In fact, we are faced with nothing here but a particular application of the principle of diminishing returns. The relationship between the prices of labor and land will be the determinant for the employment of these factors in production.

Finally, the substitution of originary factors of production, primarily labor, and capital, is possible. The common point of view assumes that (relatively) more expensive labor will be replaced by cheaper machine power[42] and vice versa. However,

---

[41] A complete equalization of prices will perhaps not occur if the necessity of employing a non-increasable specific factor of production in the production of **A** restricts the expansion of production. It is well-known that in such a case, the more expensive good can come to be considered a luxury without "objective" justification because of its higher price.

[42] There is, of course, also the substitution between labor and intermediary products: More expensive labor, or more labor, saves raw materials and vice versa.

since every capital good is simply previously expended originary factors of production, here the substitution goes in this direction: The expenditure of more labor in a briefer roundabout production process or of less labor in a more lengthy roundabout production process (by employing more capital) and vice versa. The entrepreneur calculates the possibility of substituting when calculating costs. He will employ previously done labor in the form of capital goods to a greater extent if at the given prices, i.e., in particular at the going interest rate, the earlier expenditure of labor brings a better return. For the entrepreneur, earlier employment of labor means on the one hand, an increase in the cost burden (of the labor wage) due to interest; on the other hand, however, it means an increase in output equal to the difference between the productivity of an earlier labor expenditure and that of a later one. The result here is an interrelation of the price of labor employed in the realm of consumer goods production and the labor employed in much earlier production stages, even if, because of the friction associated with reallocating labor, an equalization of wages is not possible.

These brief explanations only serve to point out that the plain model of supply and demand and the cost principle alone are not able to determine once and for all the system of prices as long as one avoids considering the changes of market configurations which arise from the relationship between presently existing prices. We merely seek to emphasize the even stronger interconnectedness of the system of prices that results from this fact. For the special purposes of our study, no further deductions are needed. If we later assume a system of prices and study disturbances in the structure of this system, we will primarily be concerned with the vertical connectivity of prices. This is related to the subject matter of our study: For the specific function of capital is the structuring of production processes in vertical stages. In an exchange economy based on division of labor, these stages will be determined by the relationship between prices. Consequently, for the analysis of capital the structure of the price system is primarily of interest as regards the relationships of preceding and succeeding prices, i.e., regarding the relationships between the prices of factors of production, capital goods, and consumer goods.

9. Marginal Productivity and the Formation of Costs. The Static System

Of all our explanations, nothing is as likely to appear as "foreign to reality" as the principle of marginal productivity. The theoretical derivation of the principle, as we have presented for the so-called law of diminishing agricultural returns, will appear reasonable as a purely "theoretical construction." It is very plausible that the increase of one of several cooperating factors of production will not lead to a proportionate increase in the output; this can only be expected from a corresponding increase in all factors of production. If one regards experience, however, then in fact the opposite relationship seems to exist in many cases. Consequently, would this be a case in which a doctrine—the doctrine of marginal productivity—is "theoretically correct, but wrong in practice?" To us the situation appears to be the same here as always whenever one believes oneself able to point out a contradiction between theory and practice: A theory can only be applied to experience as a whole. It would be wrong to believe that one could break off part of the theoretical structure and triumphantly refute it in practice. The assumptions, too, from which the reasoning set out always belong to a theory. And we must certainly keep this in mind, particularly with respect to the theory of marginal productivity. Perhaps we must even strive to formulate what we have already presented in this regard more precisely.

Let us first, however, present the various possibilities which can result and in fact have actually occurred. We will have to distinguish between three cases.

1. **Diminishing return or rising (marginal) costs**: With a given combination of factors of production the increase of one of the factors of production employed results in an increase in output which remains behind the increase in this factor of production. Accordingly, a progressive withdrawal of units of one factor of production will bring about increasing losses in output with each withdrawal of a unit. This case corresponds to the assumption on which

the doctrine of marginal productivity was based.

2. **Proportional output or proportional costs**: With an increase of one factor of production employed in a productive combination, the output will grow in the same proportion, just as with a decrease in the number of cooperating factor units it will go down proportionally.

3. **Increasing output or falling costs**: The increase of one of the factors of production working in a productive combination leads to an overproportional increase in outputs, just as the decrease in one factor of production leads to a subproportional drop in output.

These pure types can be found in various combinations. Most important will be the combination of rising and falling costs. Here, with an expansion of production the transition from rising to falling costs, as well as the transition from falling to rising costs, is conceivable. The case of proportional costs will be considered essentially as a link between these combinations. Not the entire cost curve will be relevant for the isolation of the marginal product of one cooperating factor, but rather only that section will be of importance which is relevant for all actual movements. It is in this section of the cost curve where that type which could not be integrated in the cost theory based on marginal productivity theory—the type of decreasing costs—must be located. The difficulty here lies not only in the fact that with this cost structure, marginal productivity in the sense intended here cannot be spoken of. For if all units of a cost factor whose employment is subject to this law of returns were paid in accordance with the increase in output produced by the marginal factor, this payment could be larger than the total proceeds from production. One would have to look for another principle to explain the formation of the price of a factor of production. But that is not all. For even if the price of factors of production could be explained in another way, the mechanism of the law of costs could not operate. Once loss prices arise, then according to the model of the law of costs, production should again become profitable by restricting production. If "reorganization" could only be started by entrepreneurs' refraining from individual production processes—those which bring losses—thereby raising the price on the market and simultaneously lowering costs, then this would not occur. With every restriction in production, the entrepreneur will raise his own costs even more. His interest will not be in restricting, but rather in expanding production because only in this way can he reduce his costs. And since each restriction in production means that an entrepreneur raises his own costs, he leaves it to his competitors to supply the market at lower costs. One might deduce from this relationship that falling costs make the maintenance of firms impossible in free competition and that only an amalgamation of firms would be able to carry through those restrictions in production necessary for the adaptation of the market price to production costs. Production would have to be restricted until the increased product price surpassed the increase in costs connected with the restriction in production. And this kind of cost structure—falling costs—is characteristic of many modern firms, namely whenever one does not completely take advantage of one's production capacity. It is considered a rule that an expansion of production at lower costs is possible if capacity is not fully employed, and hence that the use of additional factors of production will result in an overproportional output. Only once the firm has reached full capacity will a further expansion of production be possible, and only at increased costs. The problem thus arises in the area of the falling branch of the cost curve, and this difficulty will occur with great frequency. The reason for this kind of cost structure can be found in the large investment of fixed capital which, whenever production is restricted, results in the general expenses ("the cost of the firm's readiness") being divided up among a smaller production quantum. Consequently, a reduction in costs by increasing production is possible as long as these investments permit the proportional expansion without adding cost expenditures other than the costs for material and "productive" labor.

One must certainly admit that such a cost structure is very frequent. The question is only how under these circumstances the doctrine of marginal productivity can be applied. We will only be able to arrive at a satisfactory answer here if we reach clarity regarding a few points concerning the *method* of economic theorizing.

Let us assume, using a highly "construed" example that in a closed economy in which falling costs normally do not occur and in which even those firms that have a span of falling costs in their cost structure are employed in a region of rising costs—that is, in an economy in which otherwise the law of costs functions smoothly—there are ten large automobile firms that have falling costs. These firms function such that a further expansion of production would reduce their costs. These firms assume thereby that the prices are already loss prices and that precisely because of the structure of costs, no firm is in the position of restricting production. By limiting production, each firm would only increase its costs. The other firms would not limit their production, and each firm which limited production would only benefit a competitor and hurt itself. Now, for the sake of theoretical analysis, let's make an assumption which can never exist in reality. We will imagine that these firms are suddenly transformed such that in each firm the principle of marginal productivity can take effect immediately. As impossible as this is, it is not difficult to see what would have to happen. For it is characteristic of each of these firms that they work at a loss, but that limiting those factors of production which are in fact variable, i.e., limiting the use of "productive" labor and the raw material iron (ignoring the others) cannot help. Hence this limitation must be attempted regarding other factors of production, such as invested capital, machinery, "previous labor," and previously invested iron. Now it is technically impossible to withdraw these factors of production— the machines cannot be transformed back into iron, into unexpended labor—at least not so that these factors of production are available in the form in which they previously had been. But let us imagine that a miracle had transformed the invested factors of production so that this industry's situation would immediately change. Old investments would be withdrawn from the firms, for in these productive combinations they do not bring any return[43]; they

---

[43]Their discounted return value would be equal to zero, and insofar as another use cannot be considered for them and no later output can be expected, they would have to be considered worthless. In other words, insofar as no change can be expected, the stocks of a firm operating with falling costs could only represent the

operate at a loss, while elsewhere in the economy they could bring a return. The invested capital in particular could be used at the current interest rate (or with practically insignificant pressure on this interest rate) by other firms. Production in this "overcapitalized" branch of industry[44] would be changed by withdrawing fixed capital. Withdrawing previously invested capital is thereby possible with two different effects. Either the capital is withdrawn entirely from some of the ten automobile factories and fewer firms will then exist while others are dissolved, or in each of these firms a portion of the invested capital can be withdrawn so that all of the firms continue to operate on a more limited scale. Regardless of which of these paths is chosen, whether ten smaller firms or five large firms remain,[45] the result will be a reduction

---

"liquidation value" of the investments. In practice, however, one only too often makes the mistake of calculating with cost values instead of with the value of the discounted return.

[44]It is clear that there can be overcapitalization regarding a branch of industry, i.e., regarding a more or less large part of production, but never with regard to the whole production process. Overcapitalization means here that so much capital is invested in fixed equipment that full utilization of capacity, i.e., an expansion of production to the point where costs no longer fall, is not possible because in the entire economic system there is no cost covering demand, i.e., a demand which at this production level pays a price for every individual article thrown onto the market. Thus, here overcapitalization is an incorrect investment of capital in relation to the structure of demand. However, general overcapitalization is impossible as a result of the circulatory nature of the economy: Each productive achievement can expect a complementary return from the product and itself creates the demand for whatever it produces. It is only a question of whether what that demand is prepared to assume has been produced. That the product is often only finished long after the factor of production is employed plays no role here because with a "correct" structuring of production, a corresponding subsistence fund must be given for the interim. It can never become a problem that in general too much has been produced as long as an expansion of need satisfaction is possible. It is clear that the overcapitalization of an industry, of which we are speaking here, which can only be considered a relative one, may not be confused with an excessive tying up of free capital (overinvestment), i.e., with the direction of free capital into investments from which it cannot be freed in time, and hence, with the case where as a result of a lack of free capital, a production process cannot be completed.

[45]Both cases only mean roundabout methods of production of different lengths unless a larger firm can simply be considered as a multiplication of the small firm (with an equally long roundabout production process). The length of the roundabout production processes must naturally–via the link of prices, in particular the interest rate—be adjusted to the general structure of production with consideration for the profitability of an expansion of the roundabout method of production, especially in this line of production.

of the supply of capital of these firms up to the point where falling costs no longer exist. For as long as the costs are falling, the withdrawal of fixed capital must still be profitable. It follows from our assumptions that in the end a situation in which rising costs occur throughout will be reached, and thus with regard to all factors of production the principle of marginal productivity is effective.

Let us now draw some conclusions from this completely unrealistic example. One is immediately clear: *Under any circumstance, for the relevant section of the cost curve, a structuring of production is possible in which increasing costs occur throughout for any single factor of production.* It shall now be asked why in reality a smooth adjustment to the situation in which the law of costs based on the principle of marginal productivity takes effect does not occur; it shall be asked what the condition is which so often ties production to falling costs, in contrast to our example. It shall then also be asked whether something similar to that which the example illustrated will in the end happen in reality.

First, it is probably clear that the discrepancy between our example and reality lies only in one single condition: In the fact that the investment of free capital is a process which is physically carried out and hence cannot be reversed; in the fact that once invested factors of production have assumed a physical form they cannot be transformed unrestrictedly. If it were not for this obstacle of the physically restricted convertibility of products, if *there existed unlimited variability of factors of production, the unrestricted possibility of transferring factors of production which have assumed the form of capital goods at any chosen stage of production from one employment to another, then the principle of marginal productivity could take effect without any friction.*

But does not precisely the circumstance that fixed capital cannot be withdrawn from investment lead to the consequence that the principle of marginal productivity loses all meaning when considering a reality in which one finds a great number of production processes which are overcapitalized? Here we arrive at the second question that we brought up in connection with the presentation of our example.

The process of adapting the use of factors of production to a stratification corresponding to the principle of marginal productivity actually occurs in a real economy too. It cannot occur, as we presented it in our example, where we assumed the possibility of a retroactive transformation of investments that were made earlier. Even with frictionless movements it must occur more slowly, such that a successively progressing need for reinvestments brings about a reallocation of production factors in accordance with the law of costs. Once made investments can, of course, no longer be reversed.[46] But invested capital is never tied up for such a long period that such an investment can never be reversed. Every machine will be used up and must be replaced if production is to be maintained. However, maintaining capital investments which do not bring a return by continually introducing new free capital will not be possible. Somewhere in the economy the owner of capital who wishes to expend free capital will find a possibility for an investment that will bring a profit, contrary to the presently maintained one with falling costs. An investment of durable capital that operates with falling costs will no longer be renewed once it is used up. Insofar as the entrepreneur who owns such an investment can produce any renewal fund, he will not be able to invest this in his own firm if he wishes to achieve a profit. Consequently, capital will be withdrawn from the firm and invested elsewhere. And here we see that what could happen immediately with a free convertibility of already invested factors of production—the adjustment of investments to the principle of marginal productivity—will come about slowly in the real world of restricted convertibilities in the course of the successively arising need for reinvestments to replace exhausted factors. The transformation will occur because these reinvestments are not made. Thus, the economy will move towards a state whose structure is in accordance with the principle of marginal productivity and in which the law of costs immediately takes effect through changes in the employment of factors of production. As a result of the frequent tying up of factors of production

---

[46]In a private economy, an already made investment can occasionally be reversed by exchanging it for a liquid asset—for example, by selling individual machines—whereby in general significant losses will probably have to be incurred. With the dissolution of a firm, an "organizational value" is lost.

in fixed investments, the law of costs will probably not operate such that it immediately brings about an adjustment of production. But there will be a tendency in the economy to bring about this adjustment. We can thus summarize: Tying up capital in durable investments, and hence frequently occurring falling costs, imply an important friction in the operation of the law of costs based on the principle of marginal productivity. This friction does not suspend the effect of this law, but rather only results in this law's taking effect in a process which requires a longer period of time because it can only be effected through successive reinvestments.[47]

Ever since economic science first mentioned a law of diminishing returns, it has been beyond doubt that this law is only valid *rebus sic stantibus*, and that the adoption of a new production technique interrupts the effectiveness of the law; and hence that there can be no explanation of the course of history, co-determined as it is by changes in technology in terms of the law of diminishing returns. Instead, there can only be an explanation of its effectiveness under the assumption of given data.[48] Since we have characterized the principle of diminishing returns more generally as a principle of the cooperation between economic goods, in particular as the cooperation between free capital and originary factors of production then the restriction of *rebus sic stantibus* must naturally also be significant here. The simplest formulation would

---

[47]The economic policy which attempts to protect firms with falling costs does not realize that reinvestment in such firms means tying up capital in investments in which the return will be lower than elsewhere. Let it be pointed out here that it is characteristic of a specific stage of the business cycle that the possibilities for investing free capital are unusually limited. We will deal with this problem later. Here we are only concerned—as emphasized explicitly—with the general question of the possibility of structuring production according to the principle of marginal productivity.

[48]This restriction finds its most important application in the law of population: An increasing population must lead to pressure on the food supplies because of the increase in production cost that results if production is expanded with the additional help of only one increased factor of production (human labor), unless technical progress makes an increase in output possible above and beyond the increase of this factor of production. Apart from technical progress the effect of the law of population naturally can be neutralized also by an increase in capital exceeding the size of the population increase. Here again, we have an example of the fact that a "correct law" of theory is only "applicable" if all of the theory's assumptions are actually met.

then be: As a rule, lengthening a roundabout method of production brings about a diminishing increase in output, but technical progress can lead to a situation in which even a shortening of the roundabout method of production leads to an increase in returns. The distinction between the two possibilities for changing output does not mean that we wish to develop a classification system, which can be applied without difficulty in each individual case to explain experience, but it means instead that we wish to understand the constructive principle underlying and directing economic processes. Where there is a possibility of increasing the output without lengthening the roundabout production process, the economy will take advantage of this possibility. This is naturally not limited solely by our technical knowledge, but also by the profitability of individual production methods: The entrepreneur will not be able to employ even the technically most satisfactory method if no favorable balance in the relation between cost expenditures and revenues exists. Nonetheless, wherever a technically new production method means a lengthened roundabout method of production, the calculation of costs—and in particular the calculation of interest—will cause the adoption of a technique to be adjusted to the economic possibilities.[49] For us, however, it is significant that—entirely independent of the possibility of shortening roundabout production processes through technical inventions—with each given technology a lengthening of the roundabout production process with the effect of increasing output is possible. The problem of the structure of production, a problem which is of great importance for the economic process, lies in the limits of the economically possible length of the roundabout production processes; in the circumstances that restrict the economy in its possibility of utilizing the advantages of a lengthening of the roundabout

---

[49]Whether a new technical method—for example, the introduction of electric power—means shortening or lengthening the roundabout method of production is a question which theory cannot answer definitively in advance. The answer will depend on whether the new production method saves more capital or more labor. Consequently, the effect of new technology must not be considered only for one single stage in the vertical production structure, but for the entire course of the roundabout method of creating finished consumer goods out of originary factors of production.

production processes. Here lies the central significance of the problem of capital employment.[50]

Here, too, it can be seen that one must consider one's assumptions when applying the principle of the greater productivity of roundabout production methods to reality. It is possible to observe an increase in production with shortened roundabout methods,[51] just as one can frequently observe falling costs in modern firms. A theoretical analysis of the production process must isolate those elements from the multifarious possibilities of reality which can be used in constructing a system. The system will be applicable to, and able to offer an explanation of actual events, if it is constructed in such a way that it sets out from the principles that represent the conditions for attaining economic success which must be fulfilled in the world of experience.

We have seen this clearly with regard to the principle of marginal productivity. It would be correct for one to believe that in each individual case—for the employment of any factor of production in each individual firm—a marginal product could be established. It is not this, but something else that is the issue there: That it is possible to structure the economy according to the principle of marginal productivity, and that a deviation from this structure must cause a tendency to adjust to this structure. And with respect to roundabout methods of production, it is not

---

[50] One must refrain from confusing duration of production and length of the roundabout method of production. To again use a prior example, if an automobile factory is "modernized" with the effect of reducing the duration of production of an automobile from three months to a few days, then this is possible because machines are introduced to a greater extent. Hence, simultaneous to shortening the duration of production, an additional use of "previously done labor" takes place, and we will probably have to say that the roundabout method of production has been extended. This is so because it must be assumed that the attainment of an equivalent return with a reduced expenditure of labor has become possible because labor expenditures occur to a larger extent in preceding production stages. The temporal moving back of labor expenditure cannot be viewed solely in relation to the first finished product, but instead—with regard to the increased employment of more durable capital goods—also in relation to the products created later with this investment.

[51] It is hard to detect a shortening or lengthening of a roundabout production process in an individual case because it is difficult to evaluate the function of a single stage of production within the complex production process.

only that an extension of the roundabout methods of production can and does lead to an increase in output, but that this increase of returns is limited by the supply of capital in the economy.[52]

If starting from general principles, economic theory draws a picture of a stationary course of an economy, then it does not provide a portrait of reality. It presents a picture in which prices, product quantities and the structure of production are determined by general laws and are integrated into one cosmos. It must recognize the fact that the economy of experience can never be a realization of this model; it must admit that in the world of experience, newly arising changes in the data always keep the structure of the economy in motion. Economic theory can only present a model towards which the economy strives without ever being able to actually realize it. The cosmos of economic theory is not reality, but the laws from which economic theory is constructed nonetheless determine the real economy. Not in the sense that the real economy could never be structured other than according to these laws, but in the sense that wherever the structure of an economy deviates from these laws, wherever an economy has organized the employment of goods differently than would be required for the given data according to economic laws, a change will be initiated which has as its goal an adjustment to

---

[52]Here a brief summary is due. Whenever several factors of production cooperate, in principle various kinds of changes in the size of the output are possible by changing their combination. The possibility relevant from the point of view of economic theory, however, must be that one which corresponds to the law of diminishing returns. This follows from the fact that we are only considering factors of production that are scarce and that as a result of their scarcity must be economized. Insofar as a factor of production's cooperation in production would be subject as a rule to the principle of increasing returns, no portion of the returns could be attributed to this factor of production. For even a decrease in the quantity of this factor of production would have to be irrelevant for production. Earlier we tried to present this principle of the cooperation of scarce factors of production as the foundation of the "law of diminishing agricultural returns." The principle must be generally valid for the combination of different kinds of factors of production, but in particular also for the employment of free capital (decreasing returns with a lengthening of the roundabout methods of production). From an economic point of view, then, that which can enter into an epistemological system of the static economy is of primary relevance. Other formations of the data of an economic process can at the most be regarded separately as variations of the static course. From this point of view it was necessary for us to first consider the supply of labor in the form of an upward sloping supply curve. We tried to justify this assumption earlier.

these economic laws. Complete and certain knowledge regarding the totality of an economy is only possible through an understanding of the system. Should one do without a system because not everything in reality is structured in complete accordance with this totality? One thing in particular should keep the premature critic from doing so: Only an understanding of the system shows what the limitations of economic possibilities are and what adjustments must ensue if the economic structure deviates from this system. And once one has recognized the central importance of the doctrine of the function of capital in the structure of an economy, then one will not be able to close one's eyes to the fact that this doctrine is also of the greatest practical significance. The structure of production is identical to the employment of capital. One can safely say that this is the most sensitive element in the entire economic system. Production pushes towards lengthening roundabout production processes, and the extremely sensitive measure of interest rates indicates the possible limits. In looking at the monetary economy, we will now see just how sensitive this instrument is and how easily it can be disturbed.

Money and Capital

1. Price System and Price Level

In the static course of an exchange economy, the prices of all goods are integrated into a system according to the laws of the vertical and horizontal connectivity of prices. For this system of prices, the monetary expression of prices is completely irrelevant. When a unit of good G_1 is equal in price to 2 units of good G_2 or 3 units of good G_3, then this relationship will not change, regardless of whether the price of G_1 in money is established at 1 or 100 as long as the prices of G_2 and G_3 are one-half or one-third respectively of this price. Any multiplication of money prices is possible without thereby disturbing the system of prices as long as this multiplication occurs to the same degree for all prices. The "value" or "purchasing power" of money (the monetary unit) is then high or low, depending on how high the prices are, or—since, of course, every price is only a part of the price system—depending on how high a given price is. Any given price could serve as the standard for the height of the price level, or as an index for the purchasing power of money.

It would now be a grave mistake if from this neutrality of the system of prices of goods regarding the height of the price level one were to draw the conclusion that the problem of money is solved by answering the question concerning the height of prices. If one can assume that a specific system of prices can exist at a higher or lower level of money prices, if consequently a system of prices can be conceived of as independent of the height of prices, one must not overlook the important fact that while it is possible to think of one and the same price system as expressed through a lower or higher level of money prices, it will never (or only under very special circumstances[53] which never occur in practice) be possible to move a price system from one level to another without changing the relationships between individual prices. Yet, since in an exchange economy prices determine the allocation of the factors of production, the structure of production, and the sale of goods, every change in the level of prices must also lead to changes in the allocation of goods via a change in the price system.

This immediately becomes clear if one observes the effects of a change in the money supply. Imagine, for example, that in a static economy individual economic subjects receive an amount of money which previously was not used in the economy. These economic subjects will probably not simply keep the money, but will spend it. In other words, the economic subjects will revise their supply and demand positions with respect to their newly allotted money such that for each price under consideration they will purchase more (and under certain circumstances sell less) than heretofore. This change in demand (and supply) on the market must lead to an increase in prices.

It will never be possible to assume that this price movement will become effective to the same extent for all goods. How the new money is used will determine which goods will be in greater demand. And just as the demand reaching the market is always only the sum of individual demands, every change in individual demand will also change the composition of the total demand. An increase in demand will occur for those goods which are in greater demand, especially by those economic subjects who are the recipients of the new money. The increase in the prices of these goods might release countermovements in another area. It

---

[53]Here is a brief description of these conditions—thereby anticipating some matters that shall only be explained in detail later. Not only an even change in the supply of money of all money owners is necessary, and furthermore a stabilization of all creditor–debtor relations, but it would also have to be guaranteed that the structure of the supply of money capital would in no way be changed. In particular, the even change in all prices could only be reached if all economic subjects are informed of the change in the money supply and make corresponding adjustments in their behavior immediately.

is possible that because individual goods increase in price, those economic subjects who are *not* enriched by the new flow of money and who thus are hard hit by this increase in individual prices will not reduce their demand for these goods to such a degree that their money demand for other goods can remain unchanged; and the result of an increase in the prices of one group of goods can be that other prices fall. Thus, as a result of increasing money we can expect with certainty an increase in the individual prices of some goods; other prices might remain the same or even fall. Naturally, an increase of some or even all prices to a varying degree is also possible. For reasons of thoroughness, let it be remarked here that these movements will not only be caused from the side of demand. It can happen that an increase in money possessions puts individual economic subjects into the position of refraining from selling goods so that this circumstance, too, can lead to a shift in prices. Naturally, the changes will move in the same direction as those caused by demand.

In any case, each appearance of additional money on the market will lead to a disruption in the given price system. Once the new money has been spent and transferred from one hand to another, in a second turnover it will again affect the relationship between prices until, in the end, the process of price changing has rippled through the entire economic system. A new system of prices will form. It should be noted here that shifts in the relationship between prices arise not only during the period of transition but that a change in the new static price system as compared to the original state must also be expected.

The ultimate cause for this probably lies in the fact that each change in the possession of money must lead to a change in the distribution of property in the economy. Whoever has money can obtain goods and use them just as someone who owns real goods. If a change in the order of property relationships has occurred because of a new allotment of money (or because money has been taken away), this will also result in a change in the employment of goods. Even in the example of an exchange economy which does not use any money, it cannot be doubted that a change in the distribution of goods also implies a change in the entire economic system, and that the structuring of the economy is not only dependent on the amount of owned goods but also on the way the goods are distributed.

One could accept all of this and still be of the opinion that an excessively detailed description of possible movements was being developed here which in practice would not be of great significance. If a change in the distribution of real goods or the possession of money leads to a situation in which, for example, fewer luxury goods and more mass products or, in general, more of one good and less of another are produced, if this price rises and that falls—the one price more dramatically and the other less so—then we are faced with fluctuations in the economy which require corresponding adjustments. And yet the clarification of the relationship of which we have spoken here is of the greatest significance if we choose it as a point of departure for the discussion of a problem which arises precisely from the way money is employed in a modern economy.

The problem is that the determination of the temporal structure of production; that is, the determination of the roundabout methods of production, depends in our economic system decisively on the way in which owned money is employed. A change in the ownership of money will change property relationships such that with each shift in property a change in the demand for one or another good will occur; moreover it can be expected that a change in the possession of money will cause a change in the structure of production regarding the employment of factors of production and the length of roundabout methods of production. If it can be shown, however, that the distribution of money to individual economic subjects also determines the structure of production, then it is thereby demonstrated that the economy's supply of money is not only decisive for the price level, but that beyond this it determines the conditions for the possibility of producing finished products.

The point of departure for treating this question must be an analysis of the function of money capital.

2. Capital in the Form of Money Assets

Earlier we explained the role of capital in production such that we only considered events in the realm of real goods without paying attention to the more complicated form of these relationships which result from the introduction of money. The intention was to present the process of employing capital, which in essence can only be an employment of material goods in such a manner that the relationships within the sphere of material goods can become totally clear. We saw that a time-consuming roundabout process of production could only be described as one in which free capital, or subsistence means, are made available by their owners for production in order to "support" originary factors of production which require continuous compensation for their employment, while a return for their use could only be expected at a later time. Each use of factors of production in roundabout production means tying up free capital—its transformation into capital goods (relatively durable investments or intermediate products) from which a return can only later be expected. However, with a successful course of production, each such binding of free capital can be regarded as temporary; all invested capital will sooner or later be free again, although, especially when capital is bound up in durable factors of production, a freeing of this capital can often only be expected very late. The final freeing up of capital can only occur in the form of proceeds from the production of consumer goods. All production processes preceding this can only be maintained by continually making a portion of the proceeds from the production of consumer goods available to them. The production of consumer goods will first use part of its return to pay for the originary factors of production it employs, another share will serve to purchase raw materials and in turn make their reproduction possible, and another part will serve as a renewal fund for the fixed capital investments in the production of consumer goods and will be transferred to those lines of production which work towards renewing this equipment. And in each stage of the preceding production processes, the free capital acquired from consumer-goods production—insofar as it does not serve for the payment of originary factors of production in this very stage itself, will be distributed further back to preceding production stages until all of the free capital is accorded to originary factors of production whose employment occurs relatively early in the temporal course of the roundabout method of production. Although a lengthening of roundabout production, and thus in particular a more extensive investment of free capital in durable capital goods, occurs in the interest of increased production, there is a limit to expanding roundabout production methods due to the limitations of free capital. The interest rate to be paid for the use of free capital provides the individual entrepreneur with an indication of the possibility of expanding production. The interest rate establishes itself at such a level that all production processes possible at this rate can find a supply of free capital and all production that can no longer afford the interest must remain undone because it would not be economic. Hence, as we have shown, it is guaranteed that a roundabout method of production will only be lengthened to such an extent that a timely freeing up of capital which is required for its maintenance occurs.

This brief recapitulation of the physical process of the employment of capital should serve here as an introduction to our analysis of capital employing production in the form it takes in a money economy. In this analysis we must always keep in mind the movements in the world of real goods which in the framework of a money economy are kept in flux by the turnover of money. If a money economy calculates in terms of money and has money at its disposal, then the movements caused by money can only have an impact on production insofar as the employment of money causes movements in the employment of material goods. During the following discussion we must keep this obvious fact in mind.

In a money economy the owner of capital initially possesses a supply of money. The question now is how the money can function as capital. We can continue from what we said during our first analysis of the function of capital, where we characterized capital exclusively as supplies of means of subsistence which were employed by their owners to support roundabout methods of production. We originally had to restrict the range of capital to subsistence means, as only these are suited to provide support for the duration of production to those who have made originary factors of production available for time-consuming roundabout methods of production. Furthermore, we have seen that it is not means of subsistence as such that can be considered capital, but rather only insofar as they, too, are employed by their owners as capital, i.e., insofar as they are made available now in exchange for a later return. Thus, we have divided the function of capital in the process of time-consuming roundabout production into two complementary parts. Capital must *first* be physically capable of providing support for those who make the originary factors of production available for the duration of the roundabout production. *Second*, it must be available for the duration of the roundabout production process: It must be expended today in order to be returned only later, or—metaphorically—it must serve to bridge the time absorbed by the roundabout method of production. Now a clear perspective of the question of capital money has been gained. Money can never serve to "support" factors of production—only actually available material goods that can be bought with money can do this. However, the owning of money can make a bridging of the temporal duration of the roundabout production process possible: The owner of capital does not make natural means of subsistence available to those who provide originary factors of production for roundabout methods of production, but instead he pays them in money; and he who has received the money in turn buys the needed means of subsistence on the market. What is employed today and only paid back later is money. And insofar as money assumes the "timebridging" function of capital, one can label it monetary capital. The employment of natural means of subsistence in the function of capital by their owners is thereby eliminated. The grounds on which an owner of wealth decides not to consume his wealth but rather to use it as capital from now on exclusively concerns the possession of money. Roundabout production will no longer be "supported" by owners of capital in the sense that a subsistence fund is offered to secure a living for those offering originary factors of production, but instead it will be "financed" by a payment of money. The entrepreneur who wishes to adopt a roundabout method of production does not need a supply of material goods, of means of subsistence, but only a supply of money.

Yet, in the process of capitalist production within a monetary economy, money can function as capital only because financing a roundabout production process at the same time makes it possible to support this production process; because those who provide the originary factors of production can be satisfied with payment in money rather than a payment with real means of subsistence, since means of subsistence can be bought on the market with this money. Money capital serves the purpose of delivering the means of subsistence actually available in an economy to those who need them as support for the duration of the roundabout method of production. Even if the control of something serving as capital is not control of real goods but of money, then in a certain sense money is still the representative of material goods, and employing money as capital means that material goods will be drawn upon to support roundabout methods of production. It is now our goal to show how financing a roundabout method of production also leads to support of the originary factors of production employed in this process. We will proceed by first considering the course of a static economy.

We will assume a freeing up of capital in the production of consumer goods. The entrepreneur sells his product of finished consumer goods for money and thereby acquires control of a sum of money. Here, money capital is naturally only that part of the monetary return from sales which is not consumed as entrepreneurial profit or capital interest.[54] In the same way, only that part of the money returns is available as "money capital" for financing roundabout methods of production which is "maintained" as savings. If the entrepreneur now uses this money capital to pay for originary factors of production, then it has thereby become possible for whoever supplied the originary factors of production to buy means of subsistence. If we compare the total revenue acquired from the sale of consumer goods as it reappears on the market in the form of a demand for consumer goods with the output of consumer goods, we arrive at the following picture: Part of the monetary return is capital interest and entrepreneurial profit. The capitalist and entrepreneur each buy part of the consumer goods with the monetary income they have received. By way of financing roundabout production processes another

---

[54]Strictly speaking, in a static economy there is no entrepreneurial profit as a difference between expended costs and returns, but only an entrepreneur's wage as payment for the "entrepreneur's labor," i.e., as part of the costs. However, since the static state is always a situation that is only reached after the adjustment to a disruption, we can define it as that state in which the entrepreneurial profit is zero, whereas in the intermediate stages of adjustment it emerges as a positive (or, depending on the circumstances, negative) magnitude. For this reason we can also speak of an entrepreneurial profit here.

part of the monetary return becomes income for those supplying originary factors of production who also then enter the consumer goods market with their monetary income. This picture only presents a very simple model which will have to be enriched later in varying ways. In particular, it will still have to be asked what consequences follow from the fact that the investment of money capital does not always imply an immediate payment for originary factors of production, but instead frequently first implies the purchase of already available capital goods. We can disregard these complications for the moment. Here the simplified model shall only serve to point out a few principles important for the analysis of the function of money capital.

It must first be seen that the introduction of money in the turnover of consumer goods is nothing but a way of dividing them up for two uses that are both consumer uses, but that with respect to their function within the temporal framework of production must be categorically distinguished. Those consumer goods which are employed in support of originary factors used in roundabout methods of production serve "reproductive" consumption as was previously described: They make it possible that originary factors of production are provided with means of support now, while the product only later takes on the form of a finished consumer good. Hand in hand with the consumer good being used up goes the production of an "economic successor" to this consumer good; simultaneous to this consumption is the commencement of the reproduction of the expended consumer good. Clearly, as long as the economy runs in a static way this "economic successor" is equal in value and price to the "invested" subsistence means. This is true regarding one part of the used up consumer goods. The other part—that part of the consumer goods which is used up by entrepreneurs and capitalists—is the object of "pure consumption." This part of the consumer goods becomes the payment, so to speak, for a previously expended service; it is not a prerequisite for the adoption of a roundabout method of production. This should be beyond any doubt after the previous explanations.

What we now see here—the partitioning of the consumer goods product into reproductive and pure consumption, that is, the division of production returns into one part that functions as capital and another that does not—we have already encountered during our discussion of the economy of real goods. The difference that emerges in a money economy is first exclusively the one already mentioned repeatedly: that a subsistence fund is not employed in the function of capital directly, but that this function is taken over by owned money. What we have in our simple model is a complete parallel between the process in a monetary economy and that in the material goods economy. In the latter, those economic subjects who attain finished products—subsistence means—at the end of production will employ part of these as capital, and invest it either themselves or through a middleman. In a money economy, only money will be invested; but all owned money that is a return from the sale of a product represents a share of subsistence means, investing money simultaneously means setting aside means of subsistence for roundabout methods of production. Financing production is the same as subsidizing it. And just as in the non-monetary economy the owner of means of subsistence may decide to invest more or less than heretofore, the same can occur in a money economy regarding one's money possessions. If the owners of money invest more money, this means that they draw upon fewer means of subsistence and leave more for the support of roundabout methods of production. The same is true the other way around: less investment of money simultaneously implies the consumption of more means of subsistence by the owners of money. Accordingly, *an expansion or limitation of the investment of money capital cannot bring about a change in the size of the demand for consumer goods.*

This statement will be very important later. Here it has been explained within the framework of a very simple model, and in a different connection it will become apparent that whenever certain conditions arise, this statement can lose its validity. For this reason, the reader must again be reminded that here we began with the assumption of a static economy and only considered those changes which arise when a sum of money obtained from the sale of products is saved to a greater or lesser extent. The model of the static economy, however, shall be considered from yet another perspective.

First, let me mention a circumstance that is irrelevant for the construction of our model, but that might make the kind of analysis presented here difficult for some to understand. The entire money return from the sale of consumer goods—not more and not less—reappears on the consumer goods market and the entire output of consumer goods will be bought with this money. It follows from this that the price level at which the consumer goods are sold on the market is the same as the price level at which these consumer goods will in turn be bought by the consumers.[55] Thus, a relationship between the whole supply of consumer goods and the entire demand for these is established. Now, will the detailed composition of the social product correspond to the structure of demand regarding the various consumer goods? Will it not be possible that too much of good A and too little of good B have been produced so that the structure of demand must lead to a decline in the price of A and an increase in the price of B? This is, of course, not only possible, but it is to be expected with certainty whenever there is a shift in the relative distribution of the consumers-good output among originary factors of production on the one hand, and owners of capital and entrepreneurs on the other. For the rich man will naturally not only buy more than the poor man, but above all he will buy other things. Thus, for example, with increased savings activity to which production has not yet adjusted in its decisions about which goods to produce, it can happen that too few goods for use by the masses and too many luxury goods for the rich are produced. This will express itself in the relationship between the prices of both of these groups of goods. It is clear, however, that this situation has nothing to do with what we are concerned with

---

[55]This is, of course, a thoroughly unrealistic construction—unrealistic because the consumer goods are not sold to an impersonal market and in turn resold by it, but rather those who obtain the consumer goods from the producers are traders who, on the one hand have costs they must cover in their sales price, and who on the other hand, also practice an important function in the distribution of goods. Strictly speaking, we would have to view the exchange of the finished consumer goods on the market—in particular also the turnover from wholesale trade to retail trade—as the last stage of "production," i.e., as the last stage of that process in which the goods mature to the form in which they are taken over by consumers. This difficulty can now theoretically be bridged in such a way that we incorporate the entire trade turnover of consumer goods into our model and consider the activity of the traders as divided into that process which is the last stage of "production" and the abstractly characterized process of obtaining a product from producers and transferring it to the consumers. The merchant will receive payment for his "productive" contribution from those demanding consumer goods.

here. Here we are discussing the principle that the extent of investments is restricted by the fact that part of the means of subsistence must be made available for subsidizing them, and that in a monetary economy nothing regarding this principle changes when money rather than means of subsistence is invested. We are thus concerned with the quantitative correspondence between monetary capital and the subsistence fund, not with the correspondence between the composition of the consumer goods fund and the type of demand for consumer goods. We have shown that an "incorrect" composition of the consumer goods fund is possible. The problems that might arise from this, however, lie outside the realm of what is treated by the theory of capital.

More important for us is a question which we were able to ignore when considering our model by simplifying assumptions to the greatest extent. In contrast to the given situation of a horizontally partitioned structure of production, our assumption that the entrepreneur employs the money capital he has received from the sale of his products in its entirety directly for the payment of originary factors of production was an assumption foreign to reality. It is clear that one part—depending on the individual case a larger or smaller, but as a rule a highly significant part—of the money capital will not be employed by the entrepreneurs producing finished consumer goods for the payment of originary factors of production, but will be used instead for the purchase of capital goods; for intermediate products as well as for durable capital goods. It is easy to see that this complicated configuration need not change anything regarding the relationship between money capital and means of subsistence. If the entrepreneur producing consumer goods employs part of his money capital to buy capital goods from a preceding production stage, he thereby transfers his monetary capital to another entrepreneur.[56] For this entrepreneur, what in the hands of his buyer was monetary capital is the return from his product, just as the entrepreneur producing consumer goods receives a monetary return for his products. The same possibilities exist for the employment of these monetary returns in preceding production

---

[56]The following is a transposition of the model, which on pp. 21f. was developed on the basis of a numerical example, into the framework of the money economy.

stages as for the employment of returns from the production of consumer goods. If we assume that in this stage, too, saving will be maintained—this being a prerequisite for a static economy—then the monetary return will partially be consumed as capital interest and entrepreneurial profit. However, it will also partially be used as monetary capital, that is, it will be invested and here—as in the previous case—this means that it will be used to purchase originary factors of production and capital goods which are the output of an even more antecedent production process. The same applies to each antecedent production process. In total, we see a partitioning of the monetary returns received from the sale of consumer goods among the two elementary employments: pure consumption of capital interest and entrepreneurial profits on the one hand, and payment of originary factors of production on the other. In both cases, however, we see the final transformation of monetary returns from the production of consumer goods into monetary income which demands consumer goods. The vertical structuring of production into a chain of successive stages has not brought about a change here. The turnover of capital goods which arises from this vertical chain is an intermediate link in the process of transforming monetary returns from the sale of consumer goods into monetary income. It is entirely unimportant here how many steps this process takes. The entire process can be explained in terms of a single formula: The monetary return from a product will change hands until it is transformed into income, be it income of capital owners and entrepreneurs or income of economic subjects who sell originary factors of production in exchange for this monetary income. Just as the monetary return from the production of consumer goods is not entirely monetary capital, but instead a part of this return will be split off by the entrepreneur and used for the payment of capital interest and entrepreneurial profit while only the remainder of it functions as capital, so will a splitting off of both kinds of income also occur in the preceding stages through which money circulates when capital goods are purchased. It must be beyond doubt, however, that partitioning monetary returns from the production of consumer goods into various incomes, which exercise a demand for means of subsistence, must occur even if an intermediate stage in the form of a purchase of capital goods is inserted, and even if there are several intermediate stages of this kind.

There is only one thing that must be noted here. If entrepreneurs in the production of consumer goods employ all of their monetary capital for the purchase of originary factors of production, an immediate transformation of this monetary capital into monetary income will result. The monetary return which has been obtained from the sale of products reaches, in the next round of payment, the economic subjects who provide the originary factors of production and these economic subjects at once purchase consumer goods from whose sales the entrepreneurs' monetary capital has come. But wherever a purchase of intermediate products has been introduced between the spending of money capital by the entrepreneur in the production of consumer goods and the transformation of this monetary capital into monetary income, a turnover in the form of the purchase of a capital good is inserted—once or several times. We would like to consider this situation using a model in which for the sake of simplicity we can disregard the splitting off of capital interest and entrepreneurial profit as regards the use of monetary returns from the production of consumer goods. The entrepreneurs in the production of consumer goods (CG) obtain a return of 100 money units. Of these they pass on 25 directly to originary factors of production, while with 75 they purchase capital goods from the first antecedent production stage (I). Here again, 25 will be passed on to originary factors of production, while 50 go to a second antecedent production stage (II) of which 25 again go to originary factors of production, while 25 are passed on to yet another even earlier stage of capital goods production (III) which finally exclusively pays for originary factors of production.[57] For us a new question now arises from the fact that money capital does not immediately travel from the realm of consumer-goods production into the hands of the income recipients, but that on the way there are certain obstacles in the form of turnovers of monetary capital for capital goods which make the temporal course of the turnovers problematic. This becomes clear if in our

---

[57]It is clear that the simplification of reality to a model here does not consist simply in the fact that capital interest and entrepreneurial profit have been ignored. In reality, the movement of monetary capital never occurs in stages to be differentiated schematically, but there is a manifold branching out and reunification of various partial branches. We can ignore this here because we are only treating the problem that results from the existence of different stages in the turnover of monetary capital.

model we relate each act of payment as well as the completion of production processes to a time unit. We will assume, for example, that all purchases and sales as well as all production processes are carried out for the period of one week and the next payment occurs only at the end of one week for the demands of the following week. The entrepreneurs of consumer-goods production sell their product and immediately transfer part of the revenue to those who provide originary factors of production who—we assume—immediately purchase their weekly needs. The rest of the monetary returns of the producers of consumer goods serves simultaneously to purchase capital goods for their weekly needs. In each of the antecedent production processes, the turnover at the end of the week will be financed by the money received at the beginning of that week. At the same time, production is structured such that in the production of consumer goods, a certain amount of consumer goods are finished at the end of each week, and in every antecedent production stage just enough capital goods are finished each week as are needed in the next antecedent stage in one week. Hence, we arrive at a simplified representation of the turnover of monetary capital. The first week a sum of 25 goes to originary factors of production from the production of

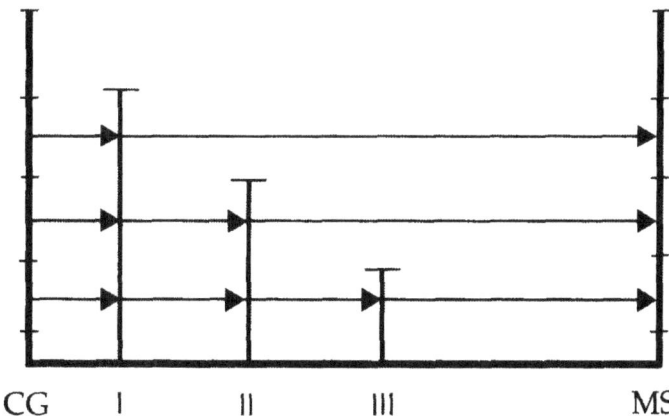

consumer goods and thence in turn onto the market for means of subsistence (MS); simultaneously, a sum of 75 goes to the first preceding production stage. The second week a sum of 25 goes from this first preceding production stage to originary factors of production, and a sum of 50 to the second preceding stage of production. In the third week a sum of 25 goes from the second stage to originary factors of production, and a sum of 25 to the

105

third stage of antecedent production, and only in the fourth week does the sum of 25 from this last stage—as the remainder of 100 units of capital expended in the first week in consumer-goods production—reach the recipients of income and from these, in turn, the consumer goods market. Of this monetary capital, one-fourth has directly—without running into any obstacles—become income, one-fourth has had to overcome one obstacle, and the other quarters have had to overcome two and three obstacles respectively. Each obstacle has tied up a share of the monetary capital for one week on its way to being transformed into monetary income for those providing originary factors of production. Clearly an undisturbed, and at all stages continuous, course of production organized in this way was only possible under the condition that in addition to the monetary capital of 100, whose passage through the various stages of production we have followed, there is still other money being turned over. It is easy to see that during the same time span in which the sum of 100 from the realm of consumer goods production becomes one-fourth income, while three-fourths is directed to the first preceding stage, a sum of 75 must be directed further from this stage: namely, 25 to originary factors of production and 50 to the second antecedent production stage. Furthermore, in the same time span a sum of 50 must be directed from the second stage—half to recipients of income and half to the third stage. Finally, in the same time span, a sum of 25 must go from the third stage directly to the recipients of income. Consequently, the economy must be supplied with money in the sum of 250 so that in this multi-stage structure, an undisturbed course of turnovers can occur, although only 100 are turned over each week in the production of consumer goods. It is also clear that those sums of money which are spent during the first week in the three stages preceding consumer goods production could only have reached these stages as the return from a previous sale of capital goods. The sums of money which run through the four stages of production will be invested in these stages as monetary capital, i.e., either for the payment of originary factors of production or for that of capital goods. Yet, that more money will be needed to maintain the "layered" production structure than will be freed up in consumer goods production is only related to the fact that—as an obstacle in the turnover of monetary capital on its way to income recipients—the purchase of capital goods is interpolated.

Our model is greatly simplified as compared to the situation in reality. It is clear that the time spans for which the purchases of capital goods occur will vary in lengths, that the renewal of capital goods will occur over varying periods of time and that the turnover of money from one stage to another will by no means always be as regular as the model indicates. Yet here we are only concerned with following the path of monetary capital in financing production and showing how monetary capital is transformed into income. And we can add to the first even further-reaching simplification we made when considering the turnover of monetary capital and clear a significant difficulty from our path. When we began with the assumption that in the production of consumer goods the entrepreneur made monetary capital available directly to originary factors of production, we conceived of the entire turnover as being carried out with a sum of money corresponding to the monetary return from the production of consumer goods. A case for this would exist in reality if, in the vertical structure of production, there were a large combination of all stages of production, including all stages from the production of the first raw materials through the completion of the finished product. Since the vertical divisions in the structure of production make it necessary that a turnover of capital goods also be financed with monetary capital, the undisturbed course of production requires a more extensive supply of money. However, it is this expanded supply of money that makes it possible—and this is what we were concerned with—that in the same time period in which an output of consumers goods is thrown onto the market for means of subsistence, a demand by the recipients of income for these consumer goods appears that can cover these means of subsistence by paying with money from their income.[58] The economic subjects

---

[58]In the graph (p. 105) each arrow signifies an exchange of money (without regard to the length of the arrow). For the sake of simplicity we have allowed the stages in the exchange of money to coincide with the stages of synchronized production. This need not necessarily be the case. One could imagine, for example, that the preceding production stages I and II are integrated and in the hand of one entrepreneur. This entrepreneur will immediately pass on 50 of the 75 units of monetary capital he has received to the recipients of income and turn over only 25 to antecedent production. The amount of money which then is needed to facilitate turnovers in the construed sequence of production is now only 200. One must keep in mind, however, that the money sum of 50 which will be paid for originary factors of production in one and the same payment by the entrepreneur integrating stages I and II finances two different integrated (synchronized) production

who appear here as recipients of income are those who make originary factors of production available and—we will again drop our assumption of an exclusion of these income expenditures—those who receive income from capital interest or entrepreneurial profit. The vertical division of production thus changes nothing regarding the relationship we recognized in our first simplified presentation.

Now we must look beyond the example of a static economy and, in a first step, include those movements which result from an increase or decrease in the supply of capital. The problem is clear: If saving occurs in a barter economy, the means of subsistence that its owner could consume and which—we are assuming a static course of the economy—in the previous sequence he did consume, are employed to support roundabout production methods. If capital is consumed, then the means of subsistence are consumed by its owner, whereas in the previous course of the economy he used them to support roundabout methods of production. In both cases, the change affects the way consumer goods are used. In a monetary economy, saving capital as well as its consumption always refers only to the ownership of money. A sum of money which in the previous course of the economy an owner himself consumed will be employed to finance a new roundabout method of production, or a sum of money which an owner previously invested will now be consumed by himself. The question again is one of the parallel between the employment of a sum of money and the economy's supply of means of subsistence. We have already addressed this briefly.

If an economic subject with control over a sum of money which he has obtained as income invests this money, this means that this economic subject refrains from consuming means of subsistence which instead go to an originary factor of production whose employment in the roundabout production process will be financed with it. In contrast, if an economic subject consumes a sum of money formerly invested in the economic process, i.e.,

---

sequences. Our model could only be so simple because we have not included the exchange of durable capital goods. However, a special explanation with regard to this exchange is not necessary. Whether the capital good purchased with money is an intermediate product (a raw material) or a durable capital good, the seller receives monetary capital which—insofar as it in turn is invested—is used to purchase capital goods or as a payment for originary factors of production.

for the purchase of a means of subsistence, this implies that financing has been withdrawn from an originary factor of production and with this, its support. Capital formation as well as capital consumption entails an increase or a decrease in the subsistence fund available for the support of roundabout production methods. Thus, the parallel between the processes within the sphere of money and the sphere of material goods is established.

3. Credit and Money Interest

In every economy there is a distribution of goods among the individual economic subjects, and this distribution of goods constitutes an economic datum. A transfer of goods from one economic subject to another through an exchange thus has the function of changing the way goods are distributed such that an economic subject receives a good for which he has a better use in exchange for another that he needs less urgently. In this sense, the socioeconomic function of an exchange is to bring about a correction in the distribution of goods without changing the distribution of wealth other than through exchange acts striving towards an improvement in provisions. With an unchanged supply of material goods in the economy each person's provisions become better when an exchange act is carried out, since each individual only engages in an exchange if he prefers it over the original distribution of goods.

If we now include those particular kinds of exchanges in the system of exchange acts which consist of trading present goods for future goods, then here too we will see a correction in the distribution of goods that has an entirely different socioeconomic function. First, it is clear that time-bridging exchange acts are by no means a necessary condition for roundabout production methods. One could easily imagine an economy in which only owners of capital appear as entrepreneurs. Individual economic subjects collect a stock of subsistence means through saving which they invest in roundabout production methods. They pay laborers with these means of subsistence (we will ignore the other originary factor of production for the sake of simplicity) and attain a large return from production, one part of which they reinvest—which in a static economy corresponds to the previously saved capital—while they consume the remainder as capital interest and entrepreneurial profit. Every exchange—including the payment for laborers—occurs step by step. One can easily imagine that production structured in this way will also be partitioned vertically, without including an exchange of present goods for future goods. The capital good will be purchased step by step from the preceding production stage with means of subsistence. One can even go one step further and imagine such a production process occurring in a money economy: The payment takes place step by step with cash. Exchanging a good for a later return, in particular exchanging currently available money for a later return (i.e., credit) is in no way a necessary condition for an economy based on division of labor employing roundabout production methods. In this, too, the exchange can be restricted to correcting the distribution of property in the sense that individual economic subjects exchange what they have step by step for something they need more urgently: Laborers exchange their labor for immediate payment, the owner of capital goods sells these for cash, the producer of consumer goods also sells for immediate payment and, finally, those who function in general as entrepreneurs purchase originary and produced factors of production for cash, just as they sell products for cash. However, it is now clear that under these circumstances the assumption of the entrepreneurial function is tied to the possession of wealth. Only he who owns wealth—either a means of subsistence that can serve as free capital, other goods that can be exchanged for subsistence means and capital goods, or cash—can adopt a roundabout method of production. Furthermore, he who has saved capital can only let this function as capital if he invests it. The moment an owner of capital makes wealth of any kind available to an entrepreneur so that a roundabout method of production can be carried out, there is an exchange of present goods for future goods. For it is the nature of roundabout methods of production that an expenditure occurs today for which a return is available only later. A division of labor between the owner of capital and the entrepreneur only becomes possible if the owner of capital makes his wealth available to an entrepreneur for a later return, i.e., if there is an exchange of present goods for future goods.[59] This interests us

---

[59]That a legal relationship (i.e., the purchase of a bond) may obscure an economic fact is of no importance here.

here only in the form in which it actually occurs in a modern economy: as the exchange of money for a later return, as the crediting of money, or simply as credit. The introduction of credit means the possibility of correcting the distribution of property in a special sense, namely in the sense that someone who owns monetary capital that he himself cannot or does not wish to use in production can transfer this to another person who can let it "work" in production; in the sense that someone who has more capital than he presently needs for production can temporarily transfer it to someone else; and finally, in the sense that someone who has less capital than he needs for production can borrow from others to whom it will later be returned. The distribution of goods will be corrected here in the sense that the distribution of wealth will be maintained; but in maintaining the distribution of wealth, the partitioning of the assets among those who employ it or cannot employ it and do not wish to employ it in production will be changed. Clearly, the introduction of credit makes a significant increase in economic returns possible, because the interpersonal transfer of capital will make it easier to direct capital into those usages in which its return—and consequently also the return from the other cooperating factors of production—will be greater. It is clear that only a smoothly operating credit market, or one operating with the least possible friction, will provide the prerequisite for "correctly" taking advantage of the supply of capital in the economy. Finally, it is also clear that a fully developed credit market is the prerequisite for the formation of a uniform interest rate, and that only a uniform interest rate makes the reliable calculation for the use of capital possible. Although we have said that credit is not a necessary prerequisite for an exchange economy using capital, we must qualify this here by adding that the institution of credit is certainly an adequate prerequisite for a relatively developed economy using roundabout methods of production. Furthermore, let it be mentioned that here we are only interested in credit as "productive credit."

Interest, as the price forming on the market for exchanging a presently available good for a later return, in particular money interest as the price for lending money for a later return, can only arise when there is a market on which presently available goods can be traded for a later return. In an economy—as we have seen, even conceivably with a roundabout structure of production—which does not have an exchange of present goods for future goods, interest does not appear as a price. To point out an analogous case, in roundabout production in which no vertical structuring of production exists, but in which instead every entrepreneur only purchases originary factor of production and sells finished products (means of subsistence), the capital good also does not appear on the market and has no price. Nonetheless, each capital good is worth something at all times; its cost price as well as its discounted return value can be calculated. And with regard to interest, even if interest is not formed on the market because those exchange acts out of which interest can emerge as a price are not carried out, even then the value of presently available goods is greater than those only available later, because the entrepreneur can attain a greater return by using factors of production earlier. Even if interest does not appear as a price, the length of the roundabout production process is still limited by the available capital, and the calculation of interest is a prerequisite for the correct structuring of roundabout production processes. Assume the following: In an economy that knows no market on which an interest rate forms, an omniscient institution exists that announces which interest rate is the "correct" one under all given conditions and in particular given the supply of capital. The entrepreneurs base their calculation of production on this interest rate; that is, they only carry out those roundabout production processes which provide a return exceeding the expenditures of such interest payments—naturally taking into account the time the capital is tied up. The economy is apparently not subjected to any disruption arising from an incorrect choice in the length of the roundabout production process. However, if the institution announcing the interest rate erred or if the entrepreneur did not abide by the correct announcement, then severe disruptions would certainly have to be expected. Calculating with too low an interest rate would mean that too lengthy roundabout production processes would be commenced. The results of this have already been presented in detail. Calculating with too high an interest rate would mean that too short roundabout production processes would be adopted, a part of the free capital would remain unused, and the return from production would be smaller than it could be.

Now it is clear that in an economy in which a market for capital does not exist and thus the interest rate does not appear as a price, the entrepreneur will have great difficulty finding the "correct" interest rate on which he should base his calculations. However, it is also undoubtedly clear that wherever a market emerges which lets an interest rate appear as the price for exchanging present goods for future goods, this market assumes the role of that institution which in the just mentioned example prescribes the interest rate. The entrepreneur will receive capital only at this interest rate, and he will know that he can use his own capital only after taking this rate into consideration if he wants to remain successful. We must say here, however, that the example we have used of an institution outside the market that prescribes the interest rate is by no means pure fantasy. We will have more to say on this later. We will only need to change this model slightly to recognize something that is peculiar to the position of a modern central bank.

This general presentation of the function of credit and interest shall make a precise description of the static course of a "money and credit economy" possible. If we assume the complete separation of the function of the entrepreneur and the owner of capital, i.e., if the capital employed in production is always acquired by the entrepreneur on the capital market by paying interest, then on this capital market we will initially see the entire supply of capital appearing in the form of monetary capital. After the previous explanation it is clear that the supply of monetary capital is identical to the supply of previously or presently saved monetary income. The capitalist who offers capital owns money which he can either use for his own consumption or invest. And it has already been explained clearly that all monetary capital represents actually available subsistence means, i.e., that in offering monetary capital actual means of subsistence which can serve to support roundabout production methods are being made available. Accordingly, *the interest rate that forms on the market on which monetary capital is offered*, i.e., the interest rate which is just high enough so that all of the monetary capital offered will be taken up by the demand for capital—is the rate at which the entire supply of subsistence means available for the support of roundabout production processes will be directed to this use, and also the interest rate at which the length of the roundabout production processes will be directed to this use, and *also the interest rate at which the length of the roundabout methods of production is extended just so far that it can be supported with the available subsistence fund*. The monetary interest determined on the free market by the supply of money capital is the "natural" or "equilibrium" interest rate. Expressed another way: The supply of monetary capital is a supply of "real savings capital," and the interest rate at which monetary capital is absorbed on the market is simultaneously that rate which supplies the demanders of capital with actually saved capital. In other words, the introduction of money into the circulatory system of goods and the regulation of the structure of production by the monetary interest rate do not imply any disruption in the functioning of those principles which regulate the length of the roundabout methods of production.

All of this initially holds true under the conditions of the static system which we have always assumed here.[60] Now, however, we will move on to the explanation of a possible, and in practice highly important, error in the functioning of the money market when, continuing from our general characterization of credit, we speak of a particular kind of credit that can cause a correction in the distribution of property in a sense other than the one we have discussed up to now. Let it be pointed out in advance that the form in which credit is granted has in itself nothing to do with its function. The "formal purchasing power" which all owned money represents can be made available as credit in the form of cash money (currency, coins), bank notes, or money deposits (checking accounts). Now, with regard to bank notes and checking accounts, however, it is essential that their quantities can be modified without difficulty, and this modification of the supply of means of payment in the economy interests us here primarily when it is caused by an expansion or restriction in the granting of credit.

---

[60]Until now we have only deviated from the strict assumptions of the stationary economic process where we have included new savings and the consumption of saved capital in our analysis. We have seen that in these cases, too, a reallocation of money results in a parallel change in the use of goods.

With regard to credit, here we are faced with a new function we have previously ignored. Here we are not primarily interested in the effect that it has on the price level, i.e., that under otherwise equal circumstances an increase or decrease in the supply of payment must result in a rise or fall in the level of most prices—but rather in its effect on the economy's supply of capital. It is clear that influencing the supply of capital by changing the supply of money, i.e., by expanding or restricting the granting of credit, must influence the temporal structure of production—the length of the roundabout production processes. Here, in order to simplify the presentation we are only speaking of the expanded distribution of notes by the central bank. It is obvious that regarding credit expansion by other banks, the problem is in no way different.

If the central bank offers "additional" credit and thereby expands the economy's supply of money, then the initial effect of this credit expansion will be that individual economic subjects will have more money available than previously. In addition to the money that has been in circulation this money will demand goods. The wealth of those who have received the additional credit has not increased, for they must compare their monetary assets with their debts to the central bank. This idea disguises the real situation, however, insofar as it considers what today can be realized in the economy as compensated by something which only later takes effect. Such a false classification of effect and countereffect in their temporal order is not permitted if we wish to analyze the effect of additional credit, in particular with regard to the temporal structure of production. What has an immediate effect is the additional money, not the obligation to repay. And regarding the given supply of credit, the situation is one in which economic subjects appear to be supplied with money who do not own their money supply as a result of a former—as we must assume, static—economic process. Here lies the decisive criterion for what the theory must consider novel regarding additional credit.

When presenting the function of money capital in a static economy, we have always assumed that an economic subject has access to a monetary income that he can either consume or use to finance roundabout production methods. The monetary income thereby has come parallel to the creation of finished consumer goods, such that directing this money towards investment is synonymous with setting aside means of subsistence for the support of this roundabout production process. And wherever previously formed capital is set free and made available again for production this freeing-up of money capital is identical to the creation of consumer goods. The economic subject who receives the freed-up money capital in turn has the choice of consuming these means of subsistence himself, or of continuing his previous saving and thereby making these subsistence means available for the support of roundabout production methods. It is only because free monetary capital always has an equivalent in the form of subsistence that we could conclude that financing a roundabout production method simultaneously supports the same, and hence, that the adjustments of production to the supply of saved material goods occurs through the mechanism of the money market, the formation of a monetary interest rate and its regulation of roundabout production methods. In the case we are now considering, the situation is different: When additional credit is granted, the money thereby made available to the economy provides the *possibility of financing production processes without there simultaneously being that support for production which automatically occurs with the investment of savings capital.*

We are only interested here in additional credit the central bank gives insofar as it is productive credit, i.e., credit which makes the financing of production possible. For this reason, credit is only of interest to us as it appears on the capital market—on that market on which otherwise monetary capital created by savings is offered in exchange for a later return and an interest rate arises from supply and demand. If we assume that additional credit appears on such an existing capital market, then it is clear that it will only be able to be accommodated by demand if it is offered at a rate below the ruling interest rate. The interest rate has a selective function regarding the length of the roundabout production processes, as we have already said once. If demand is now to be satisfied to a great extent, i.e., if more credit is offered, then this is identical to satisfying a demand for monetary capital previously excluded: a demand that up to now was not supplied with monetary capital because it could not pay the ruling interest rate. This demand will only be attracted by a lower interest rate, and thus an additional supply of credit can only be accommodated with a reduced interest rate. The lower interest rate makes a lengthening of the roundabout production methods possible. The limitation on the length of the roundabout production methods, which until now the interest rate assured *in accordance with the supply of real capital*, is eliminated. One problem which we will later have to address arises here.

At the same time, however, the appearance of an expanded supply of monetary capital means something else. The new money will serve to finance roundabout production processes and will thereby be passed on to the originary factors of production that then appear with this money on the consumer goods market. If production is financed with additional money, then the question of supporting the expanded roundabout production processes will arise. Here we find a second problem which will later concern us.

Both problems—the effect of additional credit on the length of the roundabout production processes as well as its effect on the subsistence means market—appear in reversed forms with a restriction of credit. Let us assume that in a static economy part of production has been financed by credit which now is withdrawn and the money used to pay back the credit is no longer spent. Here, too, shifts in the structure of production will be observable that we will later have to discuss.

Before we go on to those questions, let us present yet another point. The analysis of the static economy we previously presented when considering the money economy started from the assumption of a rigid money supply. We assumed a given supply of money in the economy: the available money appears repeatedly in the hands of the entrepreneurs who use part of the money they receive to finance production, i.e., as capital. Additional money would have a disruptive effect, as would removing money from the economy. We must, however, deviate from this consequence if we look beyond the simple model and consider the more complex situation of the modern economy. Here the question is whether the rigid money supply is a prerequisite for the fact that from the money side no disruption in the structure of production occurs. And here we must consider certain possibilities we previously ignored. Let us imagine the case in which an economic subject saves a monetary income by singly leaving money in a box. While the saver refrains from consumption, there is a reduction in the economy's potential supply of monetary capital that is equivalent to a restriction of credit. If under these circumstances the central bank replaces the money withdrawn from circulation with additional credit, then this increase in the amount of money will be a necessary prerequisite for the fact that those consumer goods which the hoarding "saver" passes up will be directed to the support of roundabout methods of production. On the other hand, if hoarded money again reaches the capital market without the central bank enforcing a corresponding restriction in credits, then this money would appear as additional money. Or, for example, let us think of those "obstacles" on the path of transferring monetary capital to the originary factors of production which exist in vertically structured production. It is easy to see that the introduction of new obstacles of this kind, through a progressive partitioning of production or a reduction of these obstacles by integration in the vertical structure, must go hand in hand with an increase or decrease in the circulation of money, unless the results are to occur which otherwise spring from a reduction or an expansion of credit.

These examples should suffice. They show that an elasticity in the volume of credit can be demanded without the adaptability of the money supply thereby leading to an interference of money in the structure of the roundabout methods of production. Let us again consider the previously presented model of an omniscient supervisory council which determines the interest rate. If the central bank could completely oversee the conditions which require the expansion or restriction of credit from the point of view of the "neutrality" of money, then depending on just such circumstances it could expand or limit credit. "Additional credit" that the central bank grants in order to compensate for the effects of hoarding are not "genuine additional credit," but "compensatory credit;" and restrictions of credit by the central bank which compensate for a "dishoarding" of money are not "genuine credit restrictions" but "compensatory restrictions of credit." However, the central bank has no reliable indicator for such a policy; there is nothing in the economy that can directly inform the central bank whether the supply of credit is greater or smaller than the supply of "real savings capital." In the money and credit economy there is no market on which an "artificial" influencing of the supply of credit would immediately lead to a disruption. Here, the rule holds that the influence on the capital market from the side of the money supply can only be recognized by the effects which credit expansions or real credit restrictions have. Even by drawing on all of the means of modern economic observation,[61] the central bank cannot arrive at that position which an omniscient institution, as we have presented it earlier, has. In practice, the central bank first sets a unilateral interest rate at which it grants credit. The magnitude of the applications which the bank receives is dependent on the height of this interest rate. If the interest rate is set at that height at which the entire supply of credit—the supply coming from the market as well as that coming from the central bank—corresponds precisely to the supply of saved capital, i.e., if each credit has the exclusive function of directing saved means of subsistence to the support of roundabout production methods, then the monetary system will work in such a way that a disturbance in the supply of capital could never come from the side of money. However, the central bank can never find a precise clue for determining this interest rate. In its discount policy it must rely on certain external indicators (reserve requirements, gold movements, the situation on the currency exchange market, etc.) As a consequence, an ideal functioning of money in the sense of a neutral money can probably never be expected—(we are ignoring that with its credit policies the central bank can also strive for another goal than the theoretical ideal of neutral money).

There is an additional point to be mentioned here. In the modern organization of credits, the central bank is not the sole source of credit. Other banks can grant additional credit—this is

---

[61]The question should be left open whether an adjustment of economic observations to this problem—there is already the start of this in the observation of business cycles—could not change something here at least in the sense that the first symptoms of the effects of monetary stimulations on the capital market could be recognized. We will have more to say regarding these effects later. This comment should, however, in no way be understood as the policy of neutral money appearing to us as the only possible policy. This must be noted here, even though there is something to be said for just such a policy. However, our interest here in neutral money is justified purely theoretically, and it would perhaps be appropriate to present this reason explicitly: In the stationary economy, monetary influences lead to "disturbances"; hence there is a question under which circumstances these disturbances do not occur, i.e., that money is "neutral." Here, the question regarding the neutrality of money is hence a question regarding the monetary conditions of the stationary course of a money economy.

the case when with unchanged liabilities banks reduce their cash reserves.[62] The central bank can never rule the money market such that it could immediately compensate for the slightest fluctuation in order to maintain the neutrality of money under all circumstances.

Thus, the problem of influencing the economy through expansion and restriction of credit results necessarily from the organization of the monetary system. The realm of the economy, however, in which we must study the effects of these disturbances in the equilibrium is the structure of production.

4. Production Under the Impact of Credit Expansion

Creating "truly" additional credit means underbidding the interest rate corresponding to the supply of saved capital. Consequently, it must lead to an excessive lengthening of roundabout production methods—to an extension of roundabout production methods beyond that limit which is justified by the economy's supply of capital. This is the basic idea underlying the following analysis. When with various modifications we repeatedly treated the theme of the "correct" length of roundabout methods of production, we thereby answered the question regarding the effects of a credit expansion. Here we can only consider the sequence of results connected with an excessive extension of roundabout production methods in the specific form it assumes in a money and credit economy. A brief reminder regarding occurrences in the real goods economy shall again serve as a point of departure.

An excessive extension of roundabout production methods must lead to an immobilization of capital investments, to a structuring of production where free capital has been invested in such a way that a timely freeing up of this capital is not possible. If the structure of "too lengthy" roundabout production methods is carried out to an end, the result will be a complete lack of means

---

[62]Insofar as a bank lends available money—in particular bank notes created elsewhere—it functions as a credit agent. Insofar, however, as a bank grants a credit that can serve as payment in the form of transfers whereby the bank simultaneously debits its clients with the credited sum, a creation of credit occurs.

of subsistence which could be used for the support of these methods[63]; the economy will have to revert to production which does not use roundabout methods, i.e., to momentary production, whereby the only qualification to be made is that the available capital goods can still be used as productive aids. In any case, the lack of free capital will make it impossible to further maintain roundabout production methods. Only that which can be produced is immediately available as a finished consumer product. If, however, the economy notices in time that a further lengthening of roundabout production methods cannot lead to a good end, then with a timely shortening of the roundabout production methods it will be able to avoid a total immobilization of capital. The economy will suffer losses, the output of consumer goods will go down and continuing provisions to the previous extent will no longer be possible, but it will be possible to maintain a roundabout production method, even if its length is reduced. In anticipation of the result of the following considerations, we can say that in general the sequence of this process in a money economy will be such that this second type of consequence of an excessive extension of roundabout production methods will occur. The expansion of credit will first make a (relatively) low interest rate possible; later on, however, a rise in the interest rate will have to be expected which forces a shortening of the roundabout production methods and *thus prevents a total immobilization of capital from making it necessary to revert to momentary production*. However, we must begin with the first effects of an expansion of credit.

Let us begin by assuming the course of a static economy in which all prices are in equilibrium and the interest rate is at such a height that it adjusts the length of the roundabout production methods to the supply of capital, and thus simultaneously causes the freeing up of capital to just the extent necessary in order to maintain the length of the roundabout method of production, and thereby also to maintain the supply of subsistence means and the stock of capital goods.

---

[63]Insofar as "durable consumer goods" are available, their productive contributions will naturally be maintained.

The investment of free capital in equipment from which a freeing up of capital can only be expected at a later point in time will occur in practice (that is, in the framework of those productions in which the formation of durable capital equipment is a particularly important form of binding capital in far-reaching roundabout production processes) with regard primarily to durable capital equipment in very early production stages. Furthermore, there will be more extended production of the raw materials needed for the production of this equipment; and finally, an increase can be expected in the stock of durable equipment in production stages closely related to the production of consumer goods or even in the stage of consumer goods production itself. However, the problem of all expanded investments is the timely freeing up of capital. Hence, our question will have to be phrased as follows: Will it be possible to set free the capital needed for the continuation of this production process in time? This question is identical to another: Will the capital fund which is generated in the production of consumer goods be large enough to make the continual maintenance of all the preceding production processes possible? Or in a more generalized version: Will it be possible to achieve a renewal fund in time at each stage of production that can secure the maintenance of all preceding production processes?

We must be aware of the fact that the continuation of this reasoning runs into a difficulty of a particular kind which is grounded in the fact that money calculation requires the translation of actual exchange ratios into money prices. If we were satisfied here with considering a real-goods economy, then according to the explanations given up to now the answer would be a very simple one: The question regarding the support of expanded roundabout production methods has been raised whereby it is beyond any doubt that the free capital, the subsistence fund available for support, has not grown. The restructuring of production must thus lead to difficulties regarding the supply of capital. However, when considering monetary calculations we must pay attention to something else. The question is one regarding the possibility of financing expanded roundabout production methods. However, with the expansion of credit more money has been made available.

Here we could now use a helpful example. We could assume that the adoption of expanded roundabout methods of production takes place without a prior expansion of credit; that is, with the previous volume of money. This is conceivable; one would simply have to assume that as a result of errors in calculations, too lengthy roundabout production methods had been introduced. It would then immediately be clear that financial difficulties would have to arise. The freeing up of money capital in the stage of consumer-goods production would not suffice to finance all turnovers that are necessary in preceding production stages. If until now the financing of production had required a specific amount of money capital, then it will now be necessary to set aside more money capital for the financing of the expanded roundabout production methods. Since this is not the case according to our assumptions, the result must be that the supply of capital will not be sufficient to satisfy the demand for capital of preceding production stages whose satisfaction is the prerequisite for the uninterrupted continuation of production. There must be a shortage of capital and a rise in the interest rate.

This model can now be applied to the case here. The first difference is that in fact more money is available. Price increases must occur. Linked with this is probably a disruption of the prior relationships between prices. More will be said on this later. However, entirely independent of the shifts in relative prices, once the additional money is turned over in an economy, a rise in prices will occur (of many or all prices, in any case—as we will later see—a rise in the prices relevant here), which means in practice that the rise in prices will compensate for the increase in the money supply. However, a surplus of money used with correspondingly higher prices to finance the expanded roundabout methods of production has the same consequences for the extent of one's financial possibilities as if an unchanged money supply would have been available with unchanged prices. The result is: In view of the price increases to be expected the increased supply of money basically means no expansion of financial possibilities. The application of our model made this clear.

Now we can clearly recognize the effects of an expansion of credit. The production processes will exercise an increased demand for money capital on the market. They will attempt to satisfy this demand partially from the revenues of their products insofar as they can split off a fund of money capital from these. Furthermore, they will enter the open capital market with their demand for money capital. The supply of capital must be assumed to be unchanged—for insofar as this capital represents a larger money sum, this is compensated for by the rise in prices. Demand has become greater—not only in its money expression, but also effectively, in the sense that in order to maintain the roundabout methods of production more capital will be required. The imbalance between supply and demand on the capital market must lead to a rise in the interest rate.

If we assume that additional credit can also be considered as a credit source, that is, that the central bank—for the sake of simplicity let us not speak explicitly of the other banks that engage in the creation of credit—offers additional credit, then an equilibration between supply and demand on the capital market is possible by creating more credit. Thus, the central bank can prevent a rise in the interest rate if it continues to grant additional credit. And here the question arises of which results must occur if the central bank continues the policy of expanding credit, if it thus prevents the relative shortage of money capital from leading to a rise in the money interest rate. The answer is quite obvious after what has already been said: Systematically stabilizing the interest rate must lead to a situation in which the "unjustified" lengthening of the roundabout production methods manifests itself with all its consequences; the excessive expansion of roundabout production then leads to a complete immobilization of free capital. With the expansion of credits, a restructuring of production is begun that leads to this final state. Only an increase in the interest rate can prevent the complete adjustment of production to "too low" an interest rate with all of its consequences. If the interest rate is not permitted to rise, the result will be a complete lack of consumer goods and a complete lack of a subsistence fund making the support of roundabout methods of production possible.

It will perhaps be helpful to present this relationship in the framework of a very simple model, whereby it shall be said in advance that this model is only a highly stylized version of reality.

We assume that the synchronized production stages are organized into six equal production stages; the expansion of credit would only influence the initiation of the last stage of the roundabout production method and hence, a reorganization of the production in the direction of a lengthening of the roundabout production methods would only occur here.[64] The newly started production stages would also begin to work using the lengthened roundabout production method. Thus, while until now each of the six production stages had lasted for a time (t)—that is, this amount of time had passed between the first introduction of an originary factor of production and the achievement of the finished consumer goods—from now on a roundabout method of production will have begun which only produces finished consumer goods at the end of a longer period of time (t+v). As long as the production stages which have left the length of their roundabout methods of production unchanged provide the economy with means of subsistence, no disruption will occur. However, as soon as the product of the last stage working with roundabout production methods of the previous length is used up, there will be a lack of means of subsistence, for the next stage of production has adopted a lengthened roundabout production process and thus cannot be finished in time. The lack of sellable means of subsistence also means a lack of freed-up money capital. If the interest rate had been raised earlier, then a shortening of the roundabout method of production would have been forced upon the lengthened roundabout production process. One thing is clear here: With this structuring of production processes the final consequence of a credit expansion with regard to the supply of consumer goods will not appear immediately, but only after a certain period of time. This time period is now characterized in our model by the fact that, initially, those production processes which are not changed in their structure make an even supply of the market with means of subsistence possible. It is only when supporting returns are required from those production processes which work with lengthened roundabout methods of production that a lack of means of subsistence will appear.

---

[64]This assumption, which we will immediately drop, is an arbitrary one. Let it also be noted that this model shall later serve in the presentation of another relationship from which the effects of a credit expansion will first be recognized in their entirety.

Let us now drop the assumption of the production process being structured in so simple a way as well as the assumption that only those production processes that are newly undertaken after the expansion of credit lengthen their roundabout method of production. It can then be clear that the lack of means of subsistence will take on a different appearance. A shortage of these will slowly arise and will assume a faster pace as the lengthening of the roundabout production method increasingly takes effect. Hence, a shortage of money capital will also gradually increase. Later we will have to take a stance concerning this relationship from a very different point of view and then arrive at a somewhat different consequence. Let one thing be said here. Since with a sequenced production structure it must be assumed that the shortage in the supply of means of subsistence (free capital) begins slowly and then will gradually increase, the possibility offered by a rise in interest rates is clear. Only an increase in interest rates can prevent an increasing shortage of means of subsistence from developing, and that in the end a complete lack of a means of subsistence emerges.

It can now be expected that in the course of the process discussed here the central bank will raise its interest rate and the expansion of credit will be discontinued before the final effects of the expansion of the roundabout production method occur. And this is so for two reasons. On the one hand, it will become apparent that the progressive expansion of credit must lead to an increasing strain on the credit system. The more the credit expansion progresses, the greater will become the share of additional credits in the overall volume of credit within the economy, while savings capital gradually loses its relative importance. Such a situation on the credit market has generally been grounds for the central bank to restrict credit. But there is a second point to be considered here. It is clear that the expansion of credit by the central bank must increase progressively if the interest rate is to be prevented from rising. For the expansion in credit simply means that *a lead in the supply of money capital over the supply of real saved capital will be created*. If with the continuing reduction in the supply of saved capital this lead is now to be maintained—with the consequence of making the same expanded length of the roundabout production methods possible—then the amount of additional money must grow more quickly with each price increase. The continuing price increase—that is, the devaluation of money—will make it impossible for the central bank to hold up to any parity of its currency or any reserve requirement. The strain on the credit system and an "endangering of the currency" will cause the central bank to raise its interest rate. And the increase in the interest rate will cause the roundabout production methods to be shortened.

Before we speak of this process, let us consider an entirely different relationship which must result from the expansion of credit. Here we must consider a process which can only develop in this way in a money economy and for which we find no equivalent in the real goods economy. Our starting point must be the specific function of money capital which we have discussed earlier: the support that it gives to production by financing it. So far we have studied the effects of expanding credit on the length of the time-oriented structure of roundabout production, i.e., above all on those elements of the production structure which are used in the early stages. Now our attention will be drawn to the end of the production process. If we have noticed above all a backward shifting of the means of production adopted in early production stages, then we will now have to ask whether or not shifts also occur in the stages of production close to consumption.

Lengthening the roundabout production methods must cause a change in the demand for factors of production. Here we wish to differentiate between two cases.

There could either be unemployed factors of production available on the market that can be purchased at the current price, or it could be that the employment of new factors of production is not possible or only possible at increased prices (and then probably only to a relatively small extent). In a different context we gave reasons for the existence of both of these possibilities when analyzing different market configurations for the area of the factor of production of human labor. Here it suffices to refer to these explanations; notice, though, that in the following discussion both of these possibilities are significant primarily with regard to human labor. In the first case the number of employed will increase without the wage increasing, and in the second case with an unchanged (or only slightly increased) number of employed the wage will increase. In both cases the size of the wage sum increases. This also corresponds to the situation which served as our starting point. With the expansion of credit new money capital is made available to the entrepreneur. This reaches the market of factors of production and thereby arises the possibility of expanded wage payments. Of course, the additional money can demand already available capital goods and thus drive up their prices. Insofar as this happens, the "obstacles" of which we have spoken appear on the path of money capital from the hand of the entrepreneur to originary factors of production. On the one hand, we must not overestimate the significance of these obstacles in this connection, because there is no reason to assume that the additional money will first reach the producer of consumer goods. In fact, just the opposite is to be expected. The production stages which are most directly encouraged by lowering the interest rate are those in which the reduction of costs due to a reduction in interest rates has a relatively greater significance, and this is most likely to be in the stages which precede the production of consumer goods in those stages in which the longest time passes between the investment expenditure and the production of the finished product. Then, however, it must be recognized that, even to the extent that the credit expansion first makes its effects felt on the market for capital goods, this alone does not cause the production structure to change. Production always needs originary factors of production in addition to capital goods, and only if there is a novel use of originary factors of production is there really something new in the economy, and not simply when the owner's title to capital goods passes from one hand to another without something new having been produced. Thus, we will summarize: The credit expansion leads to an increase in the wage sum, entirely independent of whether the number of laborers increases or not. However, the increase in the wage sum means increased demand on the subsistence means market, and hence a likely expansion in the production of means of subsistence in the sense that production will strive to meet the increased demand for means of subsistence by increasing the supply as quickly as possible.

This implies that the immediate impact of the additional amount of money on prices will first be felt on the subsistence means market via a rise in the income of those who provide originary factors of production. We have seen that the additional money must not all pass directly from the hand of the entrepreneur to the originary factors of production, but that part of this money can first serve to purchase capital goods. However, these will be capital goods which in general will be used in preceding production stages, and not capital goods that already are maturing consumer goods. In the area of consumer-goods production, the additional money will thus appear less as a cost increase but rather as an increase in demand. Consequently, we can expect an expansion of production here.[65]

An expansion in the production of consumer goods is equivalent to an increase in the fund of the means of subsistence. This makes the employment of more laborers at an unchanged wage or the better payment (a higher real income) of an unchanged number of laborers possible.[66] *However, it is of greatest importance that this increase in the means of subsistence must be linked to a consumption of capital.*

---

[65]Here a credit expansion must operate in the same way as an inflation which directly serves to finance consumption—for example, to pay for state employees.

[66]Let us briefly discuss a frequently observed situation.

1. In the case of the employment of more laborers at an unchanged wage, as long as an expansion in the production of consumer goods has not occurred, the increased wage sum will not correspond to an expanded subsistence fund. If this is the situation, we have a case of "forced saving." Hence an unchanged subsistence fund makes it possible, as a result of its higher "virulence" (reduction in the rations in which it is consumed), to lengthen the roundabout methods of production. (This would occur "at the expense" of the laborers whose wage would be less than the marginal product.) However, this relationship does not, under any circumstances, justify the possibility of a lasting "support" of expanded roundabout production methods, because it cannot be anything more than a friction. In the end, the increased wage sum will lead to an expanded production of consumer goods, lest the costs of production for consumer goods were to grow *at least in the same proportion* as the size of the money demand for means of subsistence. This cannot, however, be assumed because—as we have shown—it must be assumed that those capital goods which will first show the price increase will not be those which are intermediate products maturing into consumer goods. However, if the quick increase in the production of consumer goods is only possible through an increase in prices, the subsistence fund must grow more slowly than the size of the wage sum. If one wishes, one can also speak of forced saving here. However, certain further effects appear

Let us return again to the model of production organized into six stages we employed previously in order to consider the effect of lengthened production on the supplies of subsistence means. There we saw that lengthening the roundabout method of production in the last stage and in the newly initiated production stages would necessarily lead to a situation in which the supply of subsistence means temporarily remains constant, and a lack of these occurs only later. Now we will be able to analyze yet another change in this model. The production of subsistence means shall be increased quickly and this can only mean that capital goods which are tied up in perhaps the second or third stage of production on their way to maturing into consumer goods will be withdrawn from these stages and transformed on a shorter path into finished subsistence means. The result will be that for the following period of time an expanded supply of subsistence means may exist, but that later on there must be a greater lack of these.

Obviously, expanding provisions by expanding the production of consumer goods will never make it possible that the

---

to us to be more important, namely, that—as we will now show—in this connection *even the smallest expansion in the production of consumer goods* means consuming capital. In the other case, where a limited supply of laborers at the current wage rate lets the wages rise, the just presented idea can be applied without difficulty. Raising the monetary wage must result in a rise in real wages since the supply of means of subsistence grows. However, insofar as the prices of consumer goods increase, this rise in the real wage will not occur to the same extent as the increase in monetary wages.

2. A "forced saving" has also been derived from another connection. Wherever monetary income remains unchanged, a price increase forces consumers to refrain from consumption. One must, however, use caution in applying this rule. If, for instance, the recipient of a monetary pension is forced to refrain from consumption by a price increase, then on the opposite side there is an alleviation of a real burden on the debtor. Saving will only take place if the debtor refrains from increased consumption. However, this is in no way forced, but rather perfectly normal "voluntary" saving. (By the way, it might have its justification if one assures that the recipient of a pension will often be less inclined to save than he who becomes a debtor in order to gain larger economic successes with borrowed money. The problem, however, lies entirely in the realm of the voluntary saving.) Analogous here is the situation when contrasting the reduction in the "purchasing power" of the income of, for example, civil servants and the relief for the taxpayer. We need no longer concern ourselves here with these questions.

lengthened roundabout methods of production can be carried out to an end. For a prerequisite of any production using roundabout methods is, of course, the corresponding constant supply of consumer goods which can serve to support the originary factors of production. Here we are confronted on the one hand with an expanded provision of consumer goods, and on the other, with a lengthening of the roundabout production methods. Both of these movements work together in such a way that the expansion in provisions occurs at the expense of the supply of capital, i.e., that the consumption of capital only makes an expanded supply possible temporarily, but as a result of this consumption of capital a continuous provision will not be possible to the same extent. At the same time, lengthening the roundabout methods of production requires that the perpetual supply from the previous stock of capital lasts in order to be able to bridge the time span until the end of the lengthened roundabout production process. In a simple formula: Expanding the production of consumer goods by consuming capital will further increase the difficulties which must result from lengthening the roundabout methods of production.

When presenting the complicated relationships of the effects of a credit expansion one must necessarily make use of rather abstract models. We have been faced with the task of showing that in the structure of roundabout production two shifts will occur which as a rule must be differentiated. First, when consumer-goods production is expanded, capital will be consumed; and second, when roundabout methods of production are expanded there will be an increasing immobilization of capital investments. We could not make these two shifts any clearer other than by considering changes in various areas of a schematically structured production process. The economy of experience does not know any schematic organization of production processes. However, this cannot prevent the effects of an expansion in credit from manifesting themselves in both of the directions we have investigated. We have seen that the credit expansion gives the central bank which initiated it the option of either steadily making more credit available, or increasing the interest rate.[67] We have seen that preventing a rise in the interest rate must in the end

---

[67]It is not necessary to point out that a central bank's rationing of credit without raising the interest rate must essentially have the same results as increasing the

lead to a total immobilization of capital, but that it can be expected that the central bank will raise its interest rate earlier in order to secure the currency and restrict the credit structure.[68] With the rise in the interest rate, however, we have a new situation.

With an increased interest rate, production processes are faced with a new basis for calculation: The prolonged roundabout production methods become unprofitable. If the interest-rate increase then forces a shortening of the roundabout production methods, it thereby forces an adjustment of production to a more limited supply of capital. If the credit expansion has led to an excessive prolonging of roundabout production methods, then the halt in credit expansion leads to a liquidation of the excessive expansion of the roundabout production methods. If additional credit no longer appears on the market, then the supply of credit is identical to the supply of saved capital. Since we have no reason to assume that in this stage of credit expansion the

---

interest rate. In both cases, the extension of credit will be limited. In one case, those who are able to pay the highest interest receive credit; in the other case, some other selection principle will be decisive for the distribution of credit. Insofar, however, as a forced-down interest rate satisfies credit seekers who could not pay a higher interest, while it simultaneously excludes credit seekers who could pay a higher interest rate, a rationing of credit counteracts a distribution of credit according to economic efficiency. Besides, in view of the circumstance that in addition to the central bank other sources of credit exist, the rationing of credit will imply a lower interest only for those economic subjects whose credit demand is directly satisfied by the central bank, while elsewhere on the capital market the interest cannot be kept down unless one subjects the entire capital market to detailed restrictions with all of their ensuing consequences (which are of no interest here, however).

[68]There are only a few comments to be made regarding what would have to be expected if the central bank refrained from raising the interest rate and continued to expand credit. The progressive lack of subsistence means would lead to an emergency in the economy which would find expression in a rapid increase in prices. For reasons we have already mentioned, the volume of credit would also always increase at a faster rate. In this situation the economy would cease calculating with inflation money. However, since it is only available in a limited amount, all other money would only be obtainable on the credit market at a higher interest rate. With this, an interest rate corresponding to the supply of saved capital would take effect. During periods of great inflation, the "depreciation" of inflated money has been frequently delayed by the state's freezing prices in order to create a market in which only this inflated money could be used. In spite of this, a transition towards calculating in other currencies has often been made. In addition, when forming the interest rate for inflated money, the depreciation of money has often been accounted for by means of a corresponding rise in the interest rate.

formation of new capital by means of new saving can have any decisive impact, only the supply of capital set free in the production of consumer goods can be considered as the supply of credit. It is clear that the state of an economy depicted here only allows the freeing up of capital to a rather limited extent. Production will have to adjust to this situation. We will still have the opportunity to investigate the process of this adjustment in detail.

Let one more thing be said here. The starting point for our argument was a static economy in which a credit expansion began to take effect. Maintaining the static economy was dependent on a particular price system. The additional credit immediately caused a disruption in the price system. This disruption appeared above all in the monetary interest rate. After everything we have presented, it is clear that the interest rate in the static economic system represents a particularly important link which prevents a deviation of the various elements of this system from the path of a static course. Furthermore, we have seen that additional credits influence the relationships between the various prices by first reaching, via the originary factors of production, the consumer goods-market, forcing up the prices there. As a movement away from the static course, the expansion of consumer goods production implies consumption of capital.

Hence, increasing the supply of money by means of additional credit will not merely cause a problem of transforming one price level into another. Beyond this it will have the additional effect of disrupting the price system and distorting the structure of production.

Appendix I

On the Problem of Business Cycles

1. Prenote

There are as many causes for fluctuations in economic life as there are external conditions of economizing. Each of these conditions can change and thereby effect a change in the course of the economic process. If the economy is affected to a greater extent, if farther reaching changes prove necessary and, in particular, if a lasting change in an external determinant of the economy causes disruptions in the economy for a longer period of time, then one can speak of an economic crisis. In all of these cases, the process occurring in the economy is one of an adjustment to changed data; as compared with the smallest fluctuations which arise daily in the course of an economy, we are simply faced with a change in the dimension of the effects. However, since experience has shown that there is a certain regularity in the fluctuations of an economy—a regularity which in no way receives a satisfactory explanation from the coincidental external disturbances—one has attempted to find a specific cause for these regular cycles. Of the various crisis theories or cycle theories (since one is not only concerned with explaining a more or less "acute" crisis, but rather with a regular recurrence of upswings and downswings), today probably only those theories which can already be found in the original literary debate on the crisis problem and which look for the causes of cyclic movements of an economy in the conditions of the money market demand a right to general recognition. The following explanations, too, acknowledge the correctness of the "circulation credit theory of economic crisis," usually called monetary theory of the trade cycle.

Two circumstances speak for the fact that this theory is on the right track in the search for the cause of economic cycles. Let me first present something from experience: The process of a cyclic upswing and the development to a crisis corresponds precisely to what theory can deduce as the effect of expanding credit. Yet, there is another thing that has to do with the starting point of the theorem: When one of the magnitudes of the economic system is changed, a movement will be released that causes an adjustment of the economic system to this change. However, if the change begins with the interest rate, there is one peculiarity in this adjustment. Lowering the interest rate initiates a movement which cannot be an adaptation to data in the sense that this data will in the end be incorporated in a stationary economic course. Credit expansion occurring hand in hand with a drop in the interest rate leads to a continual movement away from equilibrium. We first presented the effects of credit expansion without regard to the crisis problem. There we saw that if they reach their final effects without inhibition, the effects of credit expansion lead to an immobilization of all capital investments. Apparently, this is a movement which does not incorporate a tendency towards equilibrium, i.e., to a stationary economic course. We have also seen that the effect of credit expansion ultimately leads to tensions so that a discontinuation of the policy of credit expansion can be expected.

We will begin with this situation in our analysis of the business cycle. Only later will we have to prove that the upswing of the cycle actually leads to a situation which is structured so as to provide the justification for our choice of a starting point.

Let it be said in advance that the method of analyzing the business cycle will be other than that which we used previously in our explanations. We can roughly describe it by saying that here we will not use the same "exact" method we applied up to now when examining the temporal structuring of production. Later we will have the opportunity to justify this change in method. Then we will see that it is necessary for the treatment of the following topic.

2. The Two Turning Points of the Business Cycle

Upon ceasing to expand credit, the state of the economy that arose in consequence of credit expansion entails the possibility that a further economic process will bring about an adjustment to the existing data. When credit is no longer expanded, the monetary element of disruption is eliminated. The only capital now available to the economy is that portion of previously saved capital that can be freed from a production process—disregarding here entirely the formation of capital through new saving. We will have to show shortly that in this situation circumstances will also arise which will prevent an undisturbed adjustment to the actual data, i.e., that will lead the economy away from the tendency towards equilibrium. Before we consider this in detail, let us first explain how such a process of adjustment to the data resulting from ceasing credit expansion would develop.

Since the supply of capital is too scarce to make possible the continuation of the already begun "too lengthy" roundabout methods of production, a discontinuation of production must result. The relatively (and probably also absolute) high interest rate will function as the selection principle for the possibility of continuing production processes. By raising the interest rate, the competition among entrepreneurs for free capital prevents those entrepreneurs who can no longer pay the going rate from continuing production. The consequence of stopping production will be the freeing up of factors of production—capital goods as well as laborers—whose prices thus must sink. After what has previously been explained, it is no longer necessary to point out that this pressure on the prices of factors of production must not necessarily lead to these prices reaching a low point at which the supply of the factors under consideration can be absorbed entirely. If in particular—and this is generally also the case when there are no price controls—a lowering of the labor wage only occurs slowly, and if it is not possible, or only possible with great difficulty, to go below a certain minimum, then greater unemployment will occur. With regard to the subsistence fund, it shall only be pointed out that the small supply of capital is identical to a reduced provision of subsistence means for the purpose of supporting roundabout methods of production. The smaller wage fund must correspond to a smaller number of laborers unless the full effect of wage pressure has correspondingly lowered the price of labor. The restrictions in production and the drop in the prices of many intermediate products will frequently result in losses. The losses of invested capital can hit not only entrepreneurs and private owners of capital but also banks that created and distributed credit. It is not necessary to present the generally known phenomenon of an economic crisis in greater detail here.

Discontinuing production processes will not occur in a systematic way. For ultimately, the course of events is determined by the actions of individual entrepreneurs who adjust to actual market conditions. In particular, the fact that the investments consist to a large extent of fixed capital equipment representing a large cost value will cause it not to come to a complete halt of already initiated production processes exclusively. Instead, the process will frequently be determined by attempts to free invested capital. Thus, factors of production will be used to finish a production process even if its lasting continuation does not appear possible. In addition to a need for free capital to continue productions, a need will also arise for capital acquired for the purpose of liquidating existing investments. If on the one hand there is now an increased demand for capital, then on the other hand a successful liquidation can mean the availability of new free capital for production. Here, too, one must note that this freeing up of capital can only occur by producing finished consumer goods; only then has an "economic" liquidation of a capital investment occurred. Wherever the liquidation only means that capital goods are being sold, we simply have the case we have repeatedly mentioned before of an interpersonal change in the position of liquidity. The prerequisite for this case is that free money capital is already available somewhere else. With regard to freeing up capital, however, let us point out yet another circumstance that arises in the course of the adjustment. A disruption of the economy might often result in production processes being continued in which new cost expenditures are justified by a corresponding revenue but in which at the same time continued production of the necessary renewal fund is not possible (or not possible to a sufficient extent).[69] Because of this, there will be a significant shortage in the supply of capital. What is significant in this respect is: The freeing up of capital does not take place to the extent necessary for the lasting continuation of production, including all necessary reinvestments. As long as a production process is continued which does not make reinvestments, the result must be disemployment in preceding production stages.

Thus, the process of adjustment which follows once the expansion of credit is halted is not at all a simple one. The demand for capital will vary according to the given situation (besides the demand expressed in order to continue production there is initially also greater demand for the purpose of liquidating production processes) as will the supply. There will be an increase in the supply through liquidation of previously invested capital, and a lack in the supply for those cases in which the production of a renewal fund is not possible and probably can only occur in the process of a readjustment of the economy. In effect, one can assume that the relatively small amount of free capital available at the outbreak of the crisis will increase in the course of this adjustment. One can assume that under these circumstances the adaptation will not occur in one uninterrupted sweep, but that there will be a longer period of continuing fluctuations. However, we have no reason to assume that a complete adjustment to the point of equilibrium—a gliding of the economy into a static economic course—would not be possible here. Regarding the interest rate, it can probably be assumed that at the beginning of the recovery from the crisis situation it will be higher and only later will slowly go down; and one can probably also assume that the degree of employment of laborers will increase with an increase in the supply of capital. The details of this movement towards a mutual adjustment of the individual elements of the economy shall not be explained further here.

---

[69]One often hears: It is only possible to cover operating costs, but not general (fixed) expenses. Achieving a return that corresponds to a previously made long-term investment is identical to the successive freeing up of this investment, i.e., with the formation of a renewal fund necessary for a static course.

However, attaining an equilibrium is dependent on one essential prerequisite, and we must now investigate whether its existence can be assumed. If we run into a new disruptive circumstance while analyzing the liquidation of the crisis, we will have to draw the consequence that the movement cannot lead to an equilibrium. Here again we are at the question of the supply of monetary capital and the height of the interest rate. The tendency towards adapting to an equilibrium can only arise under the condition of the "neutrality" of money. The prerequisite here is that the supply of monetary capital is the same as the supply of actually saved capital.[70] Ignoring the case of new savings, such real savings can only have grown out of the returns from consumer-goods production, i.e., from the freeing up of previously saved capital, with respect to which saving will now be "maintained." Wherever else monetary capital appears, it can only have reached an economic subject through the transfer of capital that is ultimately freed up in the production of consumer goods. The identity of monetary capital with saved capital here means a neutrality of money. In this sense, neutrality of money is a natural prerequisite for the crisis leading to an equilibrium. Whereas earlier we deduced the course of that process which leads to a crisis from the injection of additional credit, we will now attempt to show that in the process of liquidating the crisis a distraction from the movement towards equilibrium must be expected because money which could assume the function of capital is withdrawn from the sequence of turnovers. *Whereas we saw that in the course of the upswing a credit expansion brought about a lead in the supply of money capital over the size of the supply of saved capital,* we now wish to show *that during a depression the supply of money capital lags behind—as compared to the extent of it which would be possible according to the output of production.* Here we will first present individual circumstances in isolation that work in this direction, and only later attempt to find the link uniting them.

A first reason for the non-neutral behavior of money is already clear from the conditions that lead to a halt in the expansion of credit. The "over-straining of the credit system" will not

---

[70]Here we are ignoring another case of the non-neutral interference of money—for example, the creation of new money which will be fed directly into consumption uses—because this case is not part of the problem area treated here.

only cause the banks to discontinue the further expansion of credit, but to restrict the amount of credit they grant. In addition to this, the symptoms of the crisis—collapses and connected losses, "freezing" of credit—make it likely that the banks will make the relationship between their cash reserves and their granted credit more favorable. Hence, the volume of credit will be restricted and banks will recall cash. Something very similar can also be expected outside the area of banks: Considering the insecurity of conditions and the danger of not maintaining liquid assets—the lack of expected payments, the impossibility of withdrawing from deposits, the difficulty of obtaining credit—many firms will increase their cash reserves. As compared to the adjustment process that we have studied, all of this means a disruption in the course of an economy by withdrawing money from the circulatory system of payments.[71]

There would have been two possible ways of using this money in the economy. It could have served in the purchase of consumer goods whereby the owner of the money would have consumed it.[72] This would simply be a case of capital consumption: Previous savings were not maintained. The effects of such a procedure are not taken into consideration here. Let us notice that this situation can also occur in the course of a liquidation of the crisis; the effects of capital consumption will not be different in this special case than in any other. The other possibility open to the owner of money would have been to invest this money. This would have corresponded to the procedure in a static economy. The money would thus have been used for the payment of originary factors of production (directly from its owner or via an intermediate hand or an intermediate stage). The latter would have brought about a productive contribution and, moreover, would have purchased the consumer goods represented by this money with their monetary income. If investment does not occur here and the money is kept in the

---

[71]For the problem analyzed here it is irrelevant which type of money is withdrawn from circulation. In practice the reduction in the circulation of means of payment primarily affects check-money. On the other hand, bank notes will probably to a large extent cover payments which had previously been handled by check-money.

[72]The same would hold in the case of a consumer loan.

entrepreneurs' or banks' reserves, and a previously repeatedly granted circulation credit is no longer granted, then the demand for originary factors of production will be decreased and hence also the demand for a means of subsistence. The situation is then as follows: The means of subsistence which are waiting to be purchased by the consumers are available, but the money which should go to consumers and help them finance a purchase disappears in the course of withdrawing credit. The result will be a drop in the price of consumer goods. Here something could occur which is completely analogous to the case of the unemployed laborers in the crisis. If the prices of consumer goods do not drop to an appropriate degree—perhaps as a result of more or less narrow ties on the market—then to a large extent they will be "unsellable."[73] However, the drop in the prices of consumer goods will initiate the tendency towards restricting their production.[74]

Now the economy is in a peculiar situation. A specific amount of consumer goods has been produced and is confronted with a monetary demand which at the current prices only allows a portion of them to be taken up. The rest of the consumer goods could be available for the support of roundabout production processes, but it cannot assume this function because the money is lacking which should lead it to such use. The economy's supply of consumer goods could be an expanded supply of free capital, but the economy does not use these available consumer goods as free capital. *Finished available consumer goods form, so to speak, a potential supply of capital.* The money necessary for their purchase is there at first, but it disappears in the reserves or is "destroyed" (recall of credit), so that these finished subsistence means are neither directly supplied to consumption, nor are they drawn on to support originary factors of production used in roundabout production methods by investing this money. The

---

[73]The unsellability of a good is essentially identical to the absence of the willingness on the part of the good's owner to go below the going price. The cost-oriented thinking of vulgar economics is unable to comprehend this obvious fact.

[74]Here we have the opposite of that case which we analyzed more closely in considering the expansion of credits, namely that credit expansion leads to an increase in demand on the consumer goods market and hence spurs a tendency towards expanding this production.

result is a progressive drop in prices and a progressive shrinking of production. And a peculiar kind of situation regarding the interest rate results: The interest rate is higher than it would have to be. If for instance the lack of credit we have seen here were balanced by "a compensatory creation of credit"—as we will still see this is a very problematic thing—then the interest rate could be below that height which actually results from the supply of monetary capital. In any case, the effects of the crisis must be sharpened by this decline in monetary capital.

Let us recall here what we said earlier about the general function of capital. If in its real-goods form as a subsistence fund free capital should make the support of roundabout production methods possible, then on the one hand, it must be suitable to serve as the support for originary factors of production. But on the other hand, it must also be made available by its owner for the time period during which it is to be tied up. In a money economy, monetary capital assumes the latter function—the function of "bridging time." What we have seen here is simply that money which could assume the function of monetary capital is eliminated from economic circulation. Thus, something entirely new is brought into the process of liquidating the crisis. Whereas in our first examination the crisis had simply meant an adjustment of the production structure to a supply of capital that was too small for the present structure, now we are faced with yet another development which leads to a narrowing of the supply of capital. In our first examination we generally saw an adjustment in the area of production processes prior to the production of consumer goods. Now the effect of the crisis will also be felt in the production of consumer goods. The range of the effect of the crisis will thus be expanded considerably. The situation is probably that all of those external symptoms of the course of the economic crisis presented in detail in descriptive economics do not take effect with all their consequences through the simple process of an adjustment to a too limited supply of capital, but instead only through the effects of the reduction in the volume of credit.

It must now be shown that this situation of the economy, in particular the state of the capital market, will lead to even further-reaching disruptive moments. Something is first to be expected that is closely linked to the appearance of a reduced volume of credit which previously was the basis for our analysis. There we said that banks which are paid back credit in many cases do not redistribute this credit. However, what about those cases in the economy in which economic subjects receive a sum of money that can be invested as capital? Recalling credit by the banks is first justified essentially by the desire for an improvement in the relationship between their liabilities and their cash reserves. The increase of cash reserves by many firms can be explained in a similar way. Beyond this we will also see a desire for increased liquidity arise in another sense. Owners of capital who have invested capital in some way and are faced with many losses they themselves have suffered or that they see occurring repeatedly in the economy will generally strive to withdraw their capital from investments. This will not apply to all owners of capital, but it will occur frequently—even if not at the beginning of the crisis then in the course of the crisis—partly because capital can often only be withdrawn from an investment slowly. Insofar as owners of capital hoard money, the effects will be the same as in the earlier described case. Frequently, however, money that is withdrawn from investments is reinvested in another way: The owner of capital will no longer be prepared to make an investment of capital that can only be freed up slowly or with difficulty; "liquid" investments in the sense that the capital can be easily and surely withdrawn at any time will be preferred. The common rule is: Money will flow from the capital market to the money market. The result of a progression of this transformation will be the situation characteristic of the advanced depression known from experience: that an increased supply of short-term money credit keeps the interest rate low for this kind of capital investment, whereas capital wanted for a more lengthy investment is very expensive (or practically unavailable).[75]

---

[75]It is basically senseless to distinguish between the expressions money market and capital market. In both cases, money is offered as capital; that is, money is offered against its later return. If a short-term credit is invested in a long-term investment and if this money is then demanded back, the debtor becomes insolvent, unless another source of credit is available to him. The short-term investment in an antecedent production stage is "economically" (it would be better to say: in the global economic picture) a long-term investment since this money will only become "free" once the consumer good is complete. In a private economy, however, this money can be completely liquid if in this antecedent production

With this development, however, the economic cycle has entered a new stage. In the economic crisis, we first saw a severe lack of capital. A high interest rate reflects the imbalance between a large demand for capital arising from the continuation of too lengthy roundabout production processes and a small supply of capital. Then we saw that the lack of capital (so to speak "natural" for a crisis situation) will even grow through monetary changes. Because a withdrawal of credit occurs and higher cash reserves are maintained, a lack of money capital results. *The situation is such that the general economic conditions cause the economic subjects to change their behavior regarding the allocation of money to the function of capital.* The banks do not take advantage of the possibilities of granting credit to the same degree as heretofore. Entrepreneurs (and also the banks) seek to maintain increased cash reserves and refrain from bringing the money they have received onto the capital market to the previous extent. The result of this movement is a reduction in the amount of money employed as monetary capital for investment and a relatively larger (that is, as compared to the "economic volume") supply of cash reserves. The process of withdrawing money from the function of capital finally changes such that a transformation occurs in the way money is invested. It can probably be assumed that this change will have been preceded by an existent saturation of the economy with cash reserves and a plentiful supply of cash reserves covering credit still granted by the banks. When it no longer seems appropriate to further increase one's own liquid assets, when liquidity in the sense of a supply of cash money is already so advanced that its expansion is no longer regarded as necessary, and when the question arises of what should happen with the money capital that has become free, then in many cases a depression will bring about a specific attitude: Primarily short-term ("liquid") investments will be sought for liquid assets. In an advanced depression, a rich supply of liquid monies will be found next to a small supply of capital for long-term investments.

Here we must characterize the motivations that will become decisive in this situation in even greater detail. It must be pointed

---

stage it is possible to obtain money capital from somewhere else in the economy in exchange for one's product—from the purchaser of an intermediate product or a durable capital good.

out once again that the investment of free capital is never something that results with economic necessity from the material supplies of the economy. The situation is such that an economic subject owns money (in the barter economy: the means of subsistence), which he can either consume or invest. The choice remains with the individual economic subject and the motives which spur the individual determine the extent to which money will be offered as capital. Now it is clear that the phenomena of the economic crisis will influence the motives of the economic subjects, also in the sense that wherever capital investments are made, they will be made with greater care. Every investment means assuming a risk, and the desire to assume such a risk will probably be lower after the disruptions of the economic crisis. This applies to loaning capital by individual owners of capital as well as to the banks which, even with large cash reserves and full liquidity, will largely shy away from assuming risks. Thus, even insofar as the general conditions for the possibility of providing a supply of capital are concerned if the conditions for the appearance of a larger supply of capital are very unfavorable, then in addition the situation is one in which the objective data of the economy will not stimulate increased investment. As long as prices fall—we have already pointed out the reasons for this movement—investments are only too easily tied to losses. Putting off an investment can mean that it will be carried out at a lower cost. Anticipating the possibility of falling product prices provides yet another reason for holding back. If the uncertainty of further developments increases the danger of a loss, the owner of capital will not be very inclined to make money available to an entrepreneur; and the entrepreneur in turn will not be inclined to invest his own money or by taking on credit assume a responsibility that may become oppressive with a further decline in prices.[76]

---

[76]The risk is not only that of possible losses with falling prices. In addition, something else must be considered. Every investment generates a certain need for liquidity. This means that the investor wants to have the possibility of obtaining cash in case the fluctuations in the economy cause any changes in the assumptions on which he based his calculations. The availability of cash means in many cases the possibility of avoiding losses, often solely by virtue of the fact that one can thus wait for better times. Of course, the need for liquidity in the sense described here will vary from case to case; under certain circumstances the daring entrepreneur will also proceed without any liquid reserves. In the connection that interests us here, however, one thing must be noted: In a depression the

This situation must lead to a surplus on the money market (the market for short-term investments). Particularly for the banks, a flood of money will appear whose investment will be considered as completely liquid and recallable at any time; for logically this will frequently be viewed as the safest and most convenient form of a short-term investment. However, upon investing these short-term monies, the banks will run into difficulties, and this situation will depress the interest rate paid for these investments and under certain circumstances make it disappear entirely. This situation will lead to a further withdrawal of money from circulation if the banks see their cash reserves grow beyond their intended level.

How, then, can short-term loans of monetary capital be used in production? The expanded supply of capital will only be able to have an effect here if those production processes which permit an imminent freeing up of capital with a short production length are continuously expanded. For an economy in which there are significant investments of fixed capital, this will mean in practice that the existing investments will be used to a greater extent for current production; they will be provided with a richer supply of "operating capital"; but on the other hand, money will not be available to a corresponding degree for the purpose of investment. Even the renewal fund obtained from the revenues of production will frequently not be used for reinvestment, but instead will seek a short-term investment on the money market.

Now we have developed the theoretical analysis of the course of a depression to a point at which the disturbances gradually cease. The effect of monetary movements comes to a halt. Additional recalls of credit and additional hoarding of money no longer take place. The economy's supply of capital becomes richer, but short-term investments are preferred. With a rich supply of liquid capital, production continues, but investments, and in particular reinvestments, are greatly curtailed. With the elimination of monetary disturbances the drop in prices will

---

demand for liquid reserves will be larger, but the general abstention from investing will limit the possibilities available to every individual entrepreneur for obtaining money. This is another factor which strengthens the holding back of investments.

come to a halt. A certain degree of stability in the economy is reached.[77]

Thus, the conditions for a new upswing exist. It is clear which movement becomes the initiating force here: The wall which holds back capital on the "money market" and prevents its flow onto the capital market must be torn down. We have mentioned two circumstances that determine the situation characteristic of a depression on the capital market: the owners of capital refrain from long-term investments and the profitability of these investments with falling prices is reduced. When the absence of monetary disruptions brings the fall in prices to a halt, then it is only necessary that the psychological prerequisites for the transition to increased long-term investments, to new investments, exist; the conviction that the economy is no longer regressing must again raise the willingness for long-term investments. This willingness must exist among the owners of capital who no longer demand complete liquidity for their investments, but it must also exist among the entrepreneurs who assume credit in order to tie it up in long-term investments. As soon as a larger supply appears on the market for long-term capital investments and as soon as the investments in which an entrepreneur wants to invest appear attractive, there is a possibility for expanding production.

It is important for us here to examine in detail what will reach the market as a supply of money capital. The question again revolves around the problem of the neutrality of money. The situation here is apparently a reflection of one which appeared before the beginning of the crisis. If during the upswing an excessive supply of monetary capital surpasses the supply of real saved capital, then after the turning point, the supply of monetary capital which does not reach the potential real capital is that disruptive monetary element which prevents the adjustment towards an equilibrium. If whatever initiated the unusual movement of the depression now disappears, then we are again faced with the question of whether the ensuing adjustment will lead to an equilibrium.

---

[77]Naturally, one cannot speak of a static economic course here. The economy could not be lastingly maintained in this way because it does not reinvest to the necessary degree. Insofar as they produce capital goods for fixed investments antecedent production processes will thus be underemployed.

This would be the case if only those sums of money would appear as monetary capital which represented available means of subsistence and which were thus derived from a (newly carried out or maintained) act of saving. To the extent that only money which previously had been placed in short-term investments reaches the market for long-term capital investments, this prerequisite indeed exists. However, the conditions of the economy's supply of money will lead to a situation in which sums of money, which have not in the same sense been saved, also reach the capital market. In the course of the depression, cash reserves have been increased and credit has been withdrawn whereby the banks have achieved a significantly more favorable position with respect to their cash liquidity. Furthermore, in the course of the short-term capital investments, capital has remained temporarily unemployed, and far beyond the intentions of the economy they have perhaps led to an even greater increase in the cash reserves. Significant reserves of money are available in the economy which can be offered as monetary capital. A supply of capital can come from this which doubtless must function as additional credit. Of course, all of the money of which we have spoken here was at one time actually saved capital. Only effectively freed up capital investments have assumed the form of freely available money, and the choice of employing it as capital has remained open. Refraining from using this money for investment (or for consumption) once caused this money to be withdrawn from economic circulation: the portion of the consumer goods output corresponding to this money was not purchased with it. This loss of demand has caused a change in production. *If these sums of money that once arose from saving but were then "decapitalized" now appear as a supply of money capital, they will function to increase credit.* The same thing naturally applies in the other case, namely, in the case that new credits are granted in the form of bank deposits.

The result is that in the first movement of the upswing following the depression, a disruptive element of monetary expansion takes over—*an expansion of monetary capital as compared to the supply of real saved capital arising from the current production process.* The movement does not lead to an equilibrium but instead contains a disequilibrating element.

To be sure, the effect of additional amounts of money is not the only stimulating force in the course of an upswing. If production is expanded, if in particular favorable prices are thereby achieved, then not only will corresponding renewal funds be formed which are available as capital, but profits will also be attained which—insofar as they are saved—increase capital. This, so to speak, natural growth of capital can in itself cause an upward movement of the economy. Insofar as no more than this occurs, the movement cannot lead to a crisis; rather it can only be a movement which indicates an adjustment to a richer supply of capital. However, if in addition to this saved capital, other money appears on the market which increases the supply of capital beyond this extent, then the interest rate will thereby be held below the rate corresponding to the supply of real saved capital. An excessive expansion of the roundabout methods of production must be the consequence.

We previously presented the effect of this movement by beginning with an expansion of credit undertaken by the banks. Insofar as this formulation describes the source of additional credit, it surely is too narrow. It can probably be assumed that the banks will grant additional credit. This is because they are able to reduce their cash reserves at a time when the economy appears to be on the upswing. But in any case, "new" money will appear on the capital market from the economy. This will be that money which was previously hoarded and served to increase cash reserves. If there is great liquidity everywhere so that credit can be obtained easily, then there is no longer a reason to keep a liquid reserve in the form of enlarged cash holdings. All of this money will not reach the capital market directly; it will not all be used by the owners themselves for the purchase of originary factors of production and capital goods. In many cases it will be passed on via the banks whereby it can serve as the basis for granting more bank credit. However, for the problem at issue here it is irrelevant where the additional supply on the capital market comes from and what the ultimate sources for the nonneutral money are. What is essential is that the supply of monetary capital is not derived exclusively from savings, and hence that the interest rate will be depressed below that rate at which the length of the roundabout production processes is adjusted to the economy's supply of real saved capital.

Hence, the upswing does not lead to an equilibrium, but rather to a regular change between upswing and downswing.

3. Is the Recurrence of Crises Necessary? The Problem of Trade Cycle Policy

If we review the path we took in analyzing the moments between the two turning points in the business cycle, we find the cause of these movements in a deficient operation of those forces which adjust the structure of production—the length of the roundabout production methods—to the supply of real capital. In an upswing, an increased supply of monetary capital leads to an excessive expansion of roundabout production. If this movement can no longer be maintained and a rise in the interest rate forces the roundabout production to be shortened, a situation is thereby created which in turn leads to the withdrawal of money from economic circulation, and production arrives at a state which is the counterpart of an upswing. Saved capital is available that is not used in production, and the result is a shrinking of production which is not justified by the supply of real goods. Only the new appearance of money that had previously been withdrawn from the function of capital on the capital market leads again to an upswing, but simultaneously prevents a movement towards an equilibrium. Thus the movement leads to a new crisis.

Is this movement necessary, or is it possible to stabilize the wave-like movements of economic life? This question, which perhaps some see today as one of the most important questions of the existing economic order, leads us to examine in detail the characteristics of those elements which have an effect on the recurrence of economic cycles. Whereas we have repeatedly presented the conditions of the supply of capital as decisive for the cyclical movements, we must now point out that in these situations it is not exclusively economic necessities that are effective, but also changes in the behavior of economic subjects. This has to do with the fact that what enters the market as capital is always determined solely by people who either offer something they own to others as capital or use it themselves as capital. In the barter economy only real goods can be used as capital. There can be no more capital than there are goods actually available. If real goods are not used as capital, then they will be used up in "pure consumption," they will be available for later use or they spoil. The situation is different in the monetary economy. Capital appears in the form of monetary capital. Money received in the course of an economic transaction by an economic subject can be consumed by him or used as capital. In this case, a "monetary" disruption cannot occur. However, money can also be withdrawn from circulation. Insofar as this is the case—and it seems to us that in the course of the economic crisis this is to be expected—this withdrawal of money operates as an element pulling away from equilibrium and leading to a depression. If this money later returns to the economy, then again the movement must pass by the equilibrium and lead to a new crisis.

In this situation, the question now arises whether the intervention of economic policy could remove the deviations from the path towards equilibrium and prevent the economy from repeatedly fluctuating between upswings and downswings. The answer to this question might vary according to whether one has in mind the theoretical possibility or the chance of carrying it out in practice. From a purely theoretical viewpoint, the question can be answered in the affirmative to the extent that the theory is permitted to exclude the possibilities of changes in human behavior regarding the employment of money as capital. Wherever the expansion or restricion of the volume of credit operates as a disruptive element, a corresponding countereffect by the central bank—ignoring here again other banks[78]—can be initiated at any time. We recall here a previously used formula. If the central bank were an organization equipped with perfect knowledge regarding economic phenomena, then at any time it could secure the complete neutrality of money via a corresponding restriction or expansion of the circulation of money. Hence, it could paralyze every disequilibrating tendency resulting from monetary causes. This can occur in every stage of an upswing or a downswing. We have already mentioned that this perfect knowledge

---

[78]Ignoring the behavior of other banks here is, of course, a questionable assumption for the conditions of the economy could cause the policies of the central bank to be frustrated, at least temporarily, by the behavior of other sources of credit in the economy.

of the central bank can never be assumed, and that the central bank cannot find a reliable index anywhere in the economy on which it could base its policy. However, a certain crude interference has always been a characteristic practice of central banks: During a boom the interest rate is raised; thereby the continuation of the upswing with all of the results that must ensue when the excessive lengthening of roundabout production is allowed to run full course is halted. In turn, in a depression the central bank often tries to stimulate an upswing by granting more credit. We will have more to say about this shortly. In both cases, however, it can only be a matter of leading the economy past the two turning points more quickly—to lead it onto a path which, given the circumstances, has become a necessary one. At best, a true stabilization policy would probably begin either at the start of a downswing such that the contraction of credit will be compensated by credit from the central bank, or at an early point in the upswing so that the expansion of credit will be balanced by a restriction in the volume of money issued by the central bank.[79] This is the theoretical rule.

In practice, however, one would first have to ask how the economy would react to such a policy of the central bank. This is not solely a matter of necessary economic relationships. That the effect of an "automatic" expansion or contraction of credit in the economy could be counteracted by opposite measures taken by the central bank must initially be beyond dispute. It is only questionable whether the economy would not react in another way; namely that with such a policy of the central bank, men would change their behavior so that the policy of the central bank would be rendered futile.

Let us begin with the start of a downswing in the cycle. The here given shortage of credit has a specific socioeconomic function: It should force the entrepreneurs to liquidate the excessive lengthening of roundabout production methods. It is a healing

---

[79]That a stabilization policy should best take effect directly after the turning points is explained by the following: After the turning point, a departure from the previous development in the direction of an equilibrium is necessary. The economy takes this path. However, right from the beginning a disequilibrating element is operative, too. In any case, at the beginning of this movement, the general tendency of the economy towards equilibrium is strongest, and hence eliminating the disruptive element is most likely possible here.

force, to use a metaphorical expression. If the central bank would eliminate this result of a credit shortage by granting additional credit, then this apparently would lead to lengthening the crisis. This policy of the central bank would only mean that roundabout production methods are continued which in the long run cannot be maintained. It would perhaps be able to weaken the monetary effects of the crisis, but in the long run it would have to sharpen the crisis. For it leads from the given stage, in which production is excessively roundabout and from which an equilibrating path should be followed, on a path of continuing excessive roundaboutness of production; on a path which—unless beforehand an even more painful turnaround occurs—ultimately leads to a complete liquidation of productive investments and a complete lack of free capital. However, we said that during the development of the crisis a withdrawal of money capital from the circulatory flow of the turnover of capital also takes place within the economy because it is striving for increased liquidity and a more favorable balance of cash reserves. A compensation without damage would seem conceivable here. However, it must be clear that this compensation will not be possible because the economy will not be prepared to use the additional credit for the purpose of investment. The economy will first secure an increase in its liquidity with this credit. But there is still another thing: During the downturning segment of the cycle, the situation is such that credit for investment will be refused. With its supply of credit, the central bank will encounter a rejection of credit-taking by the economy. We have already given two reasons for this. On the one hand, the psychological conditions necessary for the investment of money into durable investments will not be present. There will be general unrest in the economy. On the other hand, the relationship of prices and the general tendency of price development will stand in the way of investment activity. The repudiation of credit will, however, not be general. Even in this stage of the cycle there is a very significant demand for credit, namely the demand by those who are forced to liquidate, to make emergency sales or to cease production due to a lack of capital—a demand for which any credit means at least the momentary avoidance of losses and perhaps even the potential for later improvements. However, satisfying this demand implies delaying the liquidation of the crisis, lengthening and strengthening it. For it is essential to this situation that a significant demand for credit by those who would like to work towards continuing the boom, that is, an "unhealthy" demand for credit, exists along with a significantly reduced demand for new sound investments.

To be sure, these explanations are highly schematic. However, they can show that the chance of a compensating expansion of credit in the recessive phase of the cycle is in practice very small; that there is hardly any chance of financing production processes which can be lastingly continued; and that the danger, instead, that additional credit prolongs and makes the crisis more severe is very large. However, if the depression is already more advanced when in the second stage of the depression there is greater liquidity on the money market, then the liquidation process is essentially completed. Hence, the danger of the damaging effect of additional credit in the just mentioned sense no longer exists. Experience shows, however that a repudiation of credit makes itself felt strongly, particularly in this stage.

Now, a cycle policy is also conceivable which, by enlarging consumption would try to avoid those effects of "decapitalization" which consist of the loss of demand for consumer goods. Here, additional money would function such that it would replace the money withdrawn from circulation and would demand consumer goods for pure consumption in its place. The movement of goods would thus be the same as if the money withdrawn from circulation had served consumption. We have already pointed out that withdrawing money from investment and using it for consumption is the same as consuming capital. Such a thing could be financed without difficulty by additional money, and the path along which this money is directed to consumption would be irrelevant.[80] In addition, some effect on the

---

[80]Financing consumption through consuming capital also occurs in what is generally recommended under the title of emergency measures in times of crises. Even though production is directly financed here, this is only done for the purpose of creating values which do not free up the invested capital. If a production integrated in the normal course of the economy is financed, then it creates a product—as we have already explained—from whose sale the further financing of this production becomes possible. If, in contrast, a street is built, then means are employed which produce a street that can naturally be valued in economic terms, too, but not a product whose sale will finance further production processes. No

relationships between prices must also surface in the form of support for the cost prices, since the pressure that the restriction of demand must ultimately exert will be weakened by this policy. Thus, the policy of financing consumption must in the end cause the emergence of price relationships that make an improvement in the potential for new investments more difficult. Regarding all this, it must finally be said that financing consumption cannot interfere at that point in the economy which (besides unfavorable price relationships) represents the decisive obstacle to carrying out new investment: namely at the psychological inhibitions which discourage undertaking new investments. The "artificially" created demand for consumer goods will ultimately also create an increased need for "operating capital" (short-term investments) and will thereby make these investments increasingly profitable. This, too, must serve to weaken the forces that work in the direction of removing the obstacles which stand between short-term investments and the long-term capital market. In conclusion let it be said that a guideline for determining the extent of credit that should operate in this way does not exist.

How is it then with an intervention by the central bank in an upswing? Could not the central bank compensate for the effect of an additional supply of capital stemming from the economy's reserves? In practice, the situation is such that a restriction of credit for the purpose of preventing or weakening an upswing would be an extremely unpopular step, in particular at the beginning of the upswing. It would probably be difficult for the administration of the central bank to justify such a step. But one

---

more shall be said here on the question of when such an expenditure can be justified solely from an economic point of view. There is only one thing to be said: If the neighbors (and other interested parties) attain a greater return after the street is built and save this return; that is, use it for new investments, then in this case the capital invested in the street is set free via a detour. If, however, this increased return is consumed, then from an economic point of view this is a case of freezing free capital. In both cases there occurs, of course, an enrichment of such interested parties at the expense of those who have provided the means for the street (or respectively in the case of inflationary money creation: at the expense of all owners of money). A purely economic calculation of profitability of the street could take place via the formula of comparing the costs with the possible surplus return for the interested parties, whereby naturally in this formula an interest rate would have to be incorporated.

must first consider the effect of this kind of policy. Let one thing be said here. The policy of a compensating credit restriction will already be a problem at the beginning of the upswing. In the economy there are significant cash reserves which gradually appear as a supply of capital. The economy's credit system is capable of expanding entirely independent of the central bank. And finally, the very first favorable production successes appearing during the upswing create new renewal capital and perhaps also new real saved capital. Where would there be a guideline for orientation for the central bank? And even if credit restrictions began, the economy would be hungry for credit, and there would be possibilities independent of the central bank. Could not a restriction by the central bank cause the speed at which additional credit is created to be increased in other ways? Once the economy's movement has been determined by the effect of a supply of capital surpassing the degree of real saved capital, once the initiation of "too lengthy" roundabout production methods has led the economy towards an economic crisis, then the only path remaining is via an economic crisis. And the only thing that remains a certain possibility for crisis policy seems to be that the central bank—insofar as it is able to restrict credit and raise the interest rate—can also force a turnaround from an upswing to an economic crisis at any time. This turning point can thus only be reached earlier than otherwise would be the case; earlier than that point at which the circumstances we mentioned elsewhere cause the central bank to halt the expansion of credit. An earlier forced turnaround would occur at the expense of the length and success of the upswing; perhaps one could hope that the severity of the crisis would thereby be ameliorated.

Whether this should be the goal of crisis policy is certainly as problematic as the question of whether cycle-stabilizing is even desirable. The call for a crisis policy is usually a call for the stimulation of production during a downswing. However, here crisis policy can lead to more general questions regarding economic policy. Whether or not it might earn a justification from any other standpoint, from the point of view of ameliorating the results of the crisis and preparing for a new upswing, everything which hampers the adjustments of economic magnitudes or impairs economic success can only be judged negatively.

4. How to Explain the Business Cycle

Economic laws can only be conceived of by assuming constant data. Once the data are given, what occurs in the economy is also precisely determined. This principle must be the basis for all economic theorizing. We applied it when we analyzed the effects that an expansion of credit must have on the structure of production. We thereby came to the conclusion that the final consequence of the constellation of data described by the formula of expanding credit must be a complete immobilization of free capital. We then tried to explain that the development will not lead to this situation, but that more often a halt to the expansion of credit will occur beforehand. We thereby introduced a new datum into our argument—in fact two further data changes: the decapitalization of money and the repudiation of credit. Finally, we also believed we could assume that decapitalization turns into a tendency to avoid or reduce long-term investments. We studied the effects of this constellation of data on the structure of the economy and thereby saw the economy advance to a lower turning point in the business cycle. Once we reached this point, we introduced a new datum—the newly appearing initiative for expanded investment which created an increase in the supply of monetary capital from the economy's reserves and additional credit.

Our argument has always had as its goal the analysis of the structure of production. The effects of the previously mentioned data constellations on the capital market were the starting point for further argumentation.

This analysis of the method we employed should show clearly how the business cycle can be explained. The people who bring the supply of capital onto the market change their behavior. This holds for the final credit source of an economy—the central bank—as well as for other banks and private owners of capital. Likewise, the entrepreneurs who make investments change their behavior. With this basis for our argumentation, we have moved outside the framework of analyzing a movement which can be explained as originating from an economic situation. In this regard there are two things to be said: First, the justification for this procedure must be given; and second, it must be shown that this procedure will not lead to incorporating any arbitrary elements.

On the first point, it is a fact that in an upswing the volume of credit grows and in a depression it falls. The monetary theory of the trade cycle is without a doubt correct in including these circumstances in its explanation. However, expanding or restricting the volume of credit can never spring from an economic law, but rather only from a change in human behavior. Thus, an explanation of the business cycle must go beyond the boundaries of an analysis applying means of economic theory exclusively.

On the second point, one could attempt to explain changes in human behavior by considering external circumstances. For example, just as the influence of regular changes in weather on harvests can be an explanation for a cyclic movement (the "sunspot theory" is methodologically possible, although it may be factually incorrect), so could there also be distant causes for regular changes in human behavior. However in our presentation we have searched for a closer link between the changes in human behavior and the occurrences in the course of a cycle. The connecting link is easy to see. *A specific economic situation* leads humans to change their behavior in a specific way. Thus, the economic crisis leads to decapitalization and credit repudiation. We are confronted with an adjustment of human behavior to a specific situation; an adjustment which certainly is no economic necessity in the sense that with the means of economic theory it could be recognized as precisely determined. Whether or not people are prepared to save, this is in any case a datum for an economic process; it is something that economic theory must assume as a starting point for its explanation. Such a fact can never be the goal for an explanation. In particular leaving money in the function of capital or newly introducing money to be used as capital—both of which we encountered in considering the business cycle—are determined by human will. But it is extremely likely that in this respect humans change their behavior in the course of a cycle.[81] If the explanation of business cycles

---

[81] In order to distinguish them from data changes which can be caused by factors entirely outside the economy I have spoken of "economically determined data changes." On this, see my article mentioned in number 8, p. 167.

wished to ignore this fact, it would neglect something that doubtlessly influences the course of events to the highest degree. We also do not believe that there is another way to solve the problem facing a cycle theory wishing to do justice to the facts: namely that the upswing creates conditions that lead to a downswing, just as these conditions in turn lead to a new upswing.

Appendix II

A Postscript on the Concept of Capital

To form concepts correctly, one must not ignore the requirement that the concepts of a nomological science can only be meaningful in respect to the statements making use of these concepts; that is, in respect to the formulation of laws. One easily gives in to the temptation of incorporating apparent similarities in one concept. Yet, when this concept is then to be applied, it becomes clear how little science can use it. Particularly regarding the concept of capital, however, the orientation towards a specific problem area is so easy to see that one really should be amazed that the not-very-glorious debate on the concept of capital could be carried on for so long.

The problem of capital arises in roundabout production. Once one recognizes that the introduction of roundabout production methods has as its prerequisite the setting aside of a subsistence fund and that the productive power of the subsistence fund limits the possibility of lengthening the roundabout production process, then everything else follows without difficulty. However, two facts have caused the problem of roundabout production methods to be completely misconceived by a viewpoint that is all too concerned with outwardly visible occurrences: the ample supply of durable capital goods and the far-reaching synchronization of production.

Because of the ample supply of fixed capital equipment, which in particular has made an ever greater shortening of the duration of production possible, one easily overlooks that a "sacrifice of time" is essential to capitalist production. We have shown that fixed capital investments are always related to the problem of free capital by the necessity of forming a renewal fund and of employing free capital as a complementary good. Only centering the question of capital on the visible capital good could permit the nonsensical doctrine of a surplus of capital to arise, and could permit the opinion to grow that an economy "too amply" endowed with capital would be capable of producing so much that sales would no longer be possible. These opinions can only be overcome by constructing a theory of capital that recognizes the problem of roundabout methods of production and takes it as its starting point. An erroneous theory of capital which views existing capital investment exclusively as the material wealth of an economy is the ultimate reason why vulgar economics as well as, in many cases, economic policy are caught up in a fetishism of the existing firm, in particular of big business. Owning capital equipment can never in itself represent wealth; it only becomes wealth if it can be integrated into the structure of production. However, if one overlooks this, if one attempts to protect the value of factory equipment even if it does not operate economically, then one invests ever more capital in a place where it is lost from the outset. Capital goods are always things that have been created and that are subject to the law of perishing. The process of the changing economy will always create new kinds of investments of capital goods if it is allowed to take its course unhindered. And if an existing investment must be lost because it does not—or can no longer—fit into the economy, then the loss is smaller than if the newly forming free capital is sacrificed to maintain what is destined to decay. However, a flawed theory of capital is also the reason for the animosity towards machines, which is again so popular these days. Machines appear to people to be something that replaces their labor and makes them breadless—no longer as something that humans have created in order to employ their labor better and more successfully. One overlooks that in the end, the use of machines only means that human labor can be used in other ways, namely in lengthened roundabout production methods. If the use of machines is "correctly" integrated in the production process, if in particular the important complementary good of free capital exists and a corresponding renewal fund can be created out of

Appendix II

the product, then the machine will not lead to unemployment, but instead to wage increases and to richer provisions.

Equally dangerous and misleading as adhering to an objectivistic concept of capital in the sense of material capital goods is the opinion that the synchronization of production eliminates the problem of roundabout production methods. If subsistence means are produced daily, then it no longer seems necessary for those working in antecedent production stages to wait until their product has matured into a consumer good; for at any time they can exchange their product for finished consumer goods. Producing more consumer goods or more factors of production no longer appears to be as difficult a problem. Earlier we encountered the question of the qualitative composition of the product, and we have seen how it can arise in the area of the production of consumer goods. The structure of the demand for consumer goods suffices to determine the "correct" composition of produced consumer goods. However, it would be a mistake to raise the question of the production of one or another product as such; that is, the question of the creation of consumer goods or capital goods—without taking into account that the mutual adjustment regarding the production of capital goods and consumer goods is the prerequisite for an undisturbed economic course. The adjustment is not only necessary such that just enough subsistence means will be created in order to support antecedent production stages. Beyond this it is also necessary that factors of production be produced in the right amount and of the right kind, so that a regular supply of subsistence means is secured. However, we are now at the problem of the length of the roundabout production methods—even for production which is synchronized to the furthest extent. The "correct" structure of production—the distribution of the supply of capital goods among stages more or less close to consumption—is dependent on the length of time necessary for the completion of production. The fact that roundabout production takes place in time and that this time is thus "economically relevant" cannot be eliminated by any synchronization. However, if one believes it possible to ignore the problem of the length of roundabout production methods and the provision of a subsistence fund because of the synchronization of production, then one must overlook everything resulting from these problems. In particular, one will not be able to recognize the consequences of choosing too lengthy roundabout production methods.

Yet, there is still something to be said here. If by capital one only understands capital goods, then something appears as capital which by its very characteristics is a capital good—something that can only be used as such. One thus ignores the important fact that the supply of capital is a problematic notion, which in turn leads to further questions. If one starts with free capital in the sense of a subsistence fund, then this does not become capital because of its material quality, but only because it is used as capital by its owner. The same is true of monetary capital. Owned money is never of itself capital, but through a particular use by its owner it becomes monetary capital. Thus, the supply of capital is always determined by a factor which lies outside pure economic ratiocination. In our analysis of the business cycle we attempted to show the immense significance of this fact.

Going beyond the realm of capital goods in the definition of capital is also necessary because only then do we have an approach to a useful concept of monetary capital. If by monetary capital one only wished to include that money which serves in the turnover of capital goods, then this would, first of all, contradict the requirements of terminological discipline: For good reasons, a much broader concept of monetary capital is needed in practice—the practitioner also knows an operating capital, a wage capital. But this alone could not be decisive. More important is that the concept of money capital must be constructed such that it leads to the problem of the length of roundabout production methods in the money economy. We believe to have made it clear that this requirement is only fulfilled if monetary capital is conceived of as the representative of means of subsistence. Only from this point of view can those movements be recognized that result when money capital takes effect as an "independent factor," i.e., when money capital and real savings capital are not identical.

We set out to describe the economic necessities which exist in the structure of production. The concept of capital with which we worked had to arise necessarily from the problem of roundabout methods of production.

LITERATURE

1. **General.** The following bibliography is limited to the most important writings from which I have set out. In all parts of this book a dependency on the works of the Austrian School of economics and those foreign-language writings that have been influenced by the Austrians or are close to them can be seen. In addition to Eugen von Böhm-Bawerk, above all William Stanley Jevons and Knut Wicksell have determined the general orientation of my investigations. I presented some basic ideas of this work in September of 1932 in a lecture before the *Wiener Nationalökonomischen Gesellschaft* and then published in the *Zeitschrift für Nationalökonomie* (vol. 5, 1934) under the title "Lohnfonds und Geldkapital"; there a few additional bibliographical references can also be found. I also had the opportunity to discuss much of what was treated here with my friends from the circle of the *Wiener Schule*. I must thank them for much valuable advice; even where I did not obtain their complete agreement, such discussions helped me to be more careful and precise in my formulations.

2. **Production and Capital.** Here one must primarily consider Jevons, Böhm-Bawerk, Wicksell, J.B. Clark, Frank W. Taussig, G. Akerman, Irving Fisher, Joseph Schumpeter and Keynes. Hans Mayer's article "Production" in the *Handwörterbuch der Staatswissenschaften*, 4th ed.; Georg Halm "Das Zinsproblem am Geld und Kapitalmarkt" (*Jahrbücher für Nationalökonomie und Statistik*, 1926); Adolf Lampe, *Zur Theorie des Sparprozesses und der Kreditschöpfung*, 1926; R. van Genechten, "Über das Verhältnis zwischen der Produktivität des Kapitals, den Löhnen und Zinsen," *Zeitschrift für Nationalökonomie*, vol. 2, 1931.

Regarding Böhm-Bawerk's theory of capital, one thing should be said here: I believe that starting with the theory of roundabout production processes requires a much closer connection between the concept of capital and the wage fund; it will thereby probably be possible to ignore the "three reasons" regarding which I must agree with those critics of Böhm-Bawerk who consider them methodologically incorrect because they cannot be incorporated in the stationary economic course. (Whoever evaluates present needs more highly than future ones will not strive for an even supply now and in the future.)

3. **Wage Fund and Wage Theory**. The literature on the wage fund theory shall only be mentioned in general. The authors cited in number 2 link the theory of capital more or less closely with the wage fund theory. John R. Hicks, *The Theory of Wages*, 1933. My *Angewandte Lohntheorie*, 1926, lacks a foundation in the theory of capital.

4. **Price System**. The discussion in the text sets out directly from the presentation by the founders of the Austrian School. On more recent formulations and problem, see for example several articles in *Die Wirtschaftstheorie der Gegenwart*, 2 vols., 1932.

5. **"Laws of Return" (the principle of the cooperation of scarce factors of production)**. Alfred Marshall still provides the best foundation. For a very instructive discussion of the newest literature see Oskar Morgenstern, "Offene Probleme der Kosten und Ertragstheorie," *Zeitschrift für Nationalökonomie*, vol. 2, 1931; Carter, *Distribution of Wealth*; Frank Knight, *Risk, Uncertainty, and Profit*; Lionel Robbins, "Certain Aspects of a Theory of Costs," *Economic Journal*, vol. 44, 1934.

6. **Money and Credit**. I have avoided discussing the general problems of the theory of money in greater detail. One should primarily name Wicksell and Ludwig von Mises, as well as the authors setting out from them. In spite of many reservations, Albert Hahn, *Volkswirschaftliche Theorie des Bankkredits*, 3rd ed., 1930, is important. (On this see Gottfried Haberler, *Archiv für Sozialwissenschaft und Sozialpolitik*, vol. 57, 1927; the same on Robertson, ibid., vol. 62, 1929.) The distinction presented in the text between the function of exchange and that of

credit follows Komorzynski, *Die Nationalökonomische Lehre vom Kredit*, 2nd ed., 1909; Fritz Machlup, *Börsenkredit, Industriekredit und Kapitalbildung*, 1931; J.G. Koopmans in *Beiträge zur Geldtheorie*, F.A. Hayek, ed., 1933.

7. **Business Cycle Theory**. Of the extensive literature on this topic, the decisive works are those which begin with the theory of credit; thus above all, Wicksell and Mises, then several of the authors named in number 2 and Spiethoff (ignoring the older ones about which, for example, Hayek speaks in his *Prices and Production*, 1931). As compared to my article "Die Produktion unter dem Einflusse einer Kreditexpansion," (Beiträge zur Konjunkturtheorie, *Schriften des Vereins für Sozialpolitik*, vol. 173, 1928), I have tried to make some changes in the formulation based on an elaborated theory of capital. Alfred Amonn, "Zur gegenwärtigen Krisenlage und inflationistischen Krisenbekämpfungspolitik," *Zeitschrift für Nationalökonomie*, vol. 5, 1934.

8. **On Method**. Setting out from a static system as the starting point of the theoretical analysis is probably common practice today. This method has special significance for us here, because we are analyzing a process that is determined by the arrangement of economic magnitudes in the course of time. An arrangement of these magnitudes that follows a single principle of construction can only be recognized if one asks the question under which conditions a process can be maintained in which the arrangement of the magnitudes over time remains unchanged. Only after considering the stationary economic course could we treat the "disruptions" in this course. Lionel Robbins, *An Essay on the Nature and Significance of Economic Science*, 1932; Mises, *Grundprobleme der Nationalökonomie*, 1933; O. Morgenstern, *Die Grenzen der Wirschaftspolitik*, 1934. The methodological orientation (which explains why the cycle theory is not—as the often cited formula of Böhm-Bawerk states—treated as a "last chapter," but rather as an "appendix" to the economic system) is developed in greater detail in my articles "Die Änderungen in den Daten der Wirtschaft," (*Jahrbücher für Nationalökonomie und Statistik*, vol. 128 [Series 3, vol. 73, 1928]). Compare also my work: *Die ökonomischen Kategorien und die Organisation der Wirtschaft*, 1923.

INDEX

(Prepared by Richard Perry)

Akerman, G., 29, 165
Amonn, Alfred, 167
Austrian School of economics, vii–xvi, xxiv

Bauer, Otto, ix
Böhm-Bawerk, Eugen von, viii, xi, xii, xviin, 1, 3–4, 16n, 165, 167
Business cycle, xix, xxiii
   contraction, 137–48
   course of, 158–60
   crises recurrence, 151–57
   expansion, 148–50
   intervention, 151–57
   problems, 135–36, 151–57
   turning points, 137–51
   see also Interest

Capital
   complimentary parts, 97
   concept of, 161–64
   constraint of production structure, 53, 60
   consumption, 74, 129–33, 141
   defined, 6
   direct exchange, 109–10
      not force of production, 2
   form of money assets, 94–109
   forms of
      fixed, 27, 34–35
      free, 27–35, 62
         complementary good, 31, 34
         consumer good frees capital, 95
         specific and restricted form, 30
         transfer between entrepreneurs, 63

   intermediate products, 27
   goods
      boom, 127–29
      consumer goods used in specific ways, 27
      durable, 14–26
   immobilization, 120–21, 131
   interest, 52–61, 109–20, 124, 126
   investment, 15–17, 23, 53
   liquid, 27, 63
   malinvestment, 121, 124–25, 132–33
   money, 2, 94–109
   as use of originary means of production, 2
   present or future, 53, 67, 110
   produced means of production, 2
   readjustments, 85
   reproductive consumption, 68
   Strigl's theory of, xx–xxiii
   supply, 61–65
   time bridging, 97
   transfer, 63
   as veil of money, 20
   wages and, 66
   see also Investments; Money; Production
Capitalism as "capitalist way," 2
Clark, John Bates, 10, 165
Consumption
   capital, 74, 129–33, 141
   consumer, 99
   reproductive, 68
Cost
   equivalencies, 52, 63
   formation, 79–90
   interest, 60
   law of, 43–46

Credit, 109–20
  contraction, 117–18
  creation of, 114–17
  devaluation of money, 127
  effect of, 120–33, 148–50
  ripple, 125
  see also Business cycle
Čuhel, Franz, vii, xii

Depression, Great, viii, xix, xxi,
Disequilibrium, 149
Durable goods
  See Goods, durable
Durable factors of production
  See Production, durable factors of

Englis, Karel, xii
Entrepreneurs
  as middlemen, 46–47, 56
  calculation and, 47, 78, 87
  competition among, 44, 57
  discovery process, 46
  in a changing economy, 85–90
  investment and, 103
  labor market and, 44
  operation of, 43, 51, 54–62, 110
  prices and, 64
  profit and loss of, 44–45, 53, 55
  technology and, 87
  see also Market economy
Eucken, Walter, xii, xv
Evenly rotating economy
  economic processes, 27–38, 89–90
  supply curves of, 40–43
Expectations
  role of, xxii–xxiii

Fisher, Irving, xviiin, 165
Funds
  derived from consumer goods, 20, 23, 25
  renewal, 11–13, 17–26, 29, 34–35, 62
  subsistence, 7–13, 18–21, 24, 26, 28, 34, 62

Gallaway, Lowell, xxin
Garrison, Roger, ixn
Genechten, R. van, 165
Goods
  complementary, 46, 70–71
  consumers', 99–106
  durable, 14–26
  money accepted as, 97–100
  substitutes, 39
  see also Capital, goods

Haberler, Gottfried von, vii, ix, xv, 166
Hahn, Albert, 166
Halm, Georg, 165
Hayek, F.A., vii, viiin, x, xi, xii, xiii, xv, xvin, xviin, xxivn, xxv–xxvi, 167
Hicks, John R., 52n, 166
Historical School, xv
Hoarding, xxii–xxv
Hoppe, Hans-Hermann, viii, xxvii
Horizontal connectivity, 37–90
Hülsmann, Jörg Guido, xviin

Interest
  credit expansion and trade cycle, 148–60
  determines length of roundabout methods, 59, 110–14
  durable goods, 61
  investment, 111–20
  malinvestment and, 59
  rate
    equilibrium, 114
    height of, 35
    natural, 114
    present and future, 113
    savings and, 65
    uniform, 58, 111
    wages and, 69–71
  reallocate production methods, 60
  see also Production
Intermediary products, 4, 14

Intervention of central bank, 151–57
Investments
    capital, 109–20
    choosing, 53
    and consumer goods demand, 100
    immobilization, 120–21
    loss, 33
    marginal product, 73
    period, 67–68
    reluctance toward, 146–48
    uncertainty, 64
    see also Capital, goods; Entrepreneurs; Interest, rate; Malinvestments; Production

Jevons, William Stanley, viii, xviiin, 3, 165

Keynes, John Maynard, xvi–xvii, 165
Kirzner, Israel M., viin, xviin
Knight, Frank, 166
Koopmans, J.G., xxivn, 167

Labor
    disutility of, 42
    marginal, 65
    mobility, 42
    as originary means of production, 1, 65
    quality of, 40
    share, 66, 68
    theory of, 65
    unemployment, 72–75
    wage fund as complementary good, 70
    wages for, 42, 66–69
    produce means of production, 3
    pushed back in time, 71
Lachmann, Ludwig, xii, xviin, xxiiin
Lampe, Adolf, 165
Land
    diminishing returns, 48–49
    as originary means of production, 1
    pension fund, 75–76
    quality of, 40
Law of returns, 46–52
Liefmann, Robert, xii
Lewin, Peter, ix
Lutz, Friedrich, xii

Machlup, Fritz, vii, ix, x, xii, xv, xxivn, 167
Mahr, Alexander, xii
Malinvestments, 15, 31–32, 59, 62, 121, 124–25, 132–33
    see also Credit, creation
Marginal productivity, 46–52, 79–90
Market economy
    function of, 109
    process, 37
    see also Business cycle
Marshall, Alfred, 166
Mayer, Hans, vii, xii, 165
Menger, Carl, xi, xii, xxii, 31
Mises, Ludwig von, vii, ix, xii, xiii, xv, xviin, xviiin, xx, xxi, xxii, xxiiin, xxivn, xxvi–xxvii, 166–67
Money
    capital assets as form of, 94–109
    cash reserves, 145
    change in quantity, effects of, 91–94
    devaluation, 127
    features of, 91–133
    holdings, 92
    market, 147–48
    non-neutrality of, 91–94, 118–20, 140
    prices, 91–94
    relation with property, 93–94
    representative of goods, 97–100
    ripple effect (new), 93–94
    supply of, 92–93
    see also Credit
Morgenstern, Oskar, vii, viiin, x, xv, 166–67

Nazis (National Socialist German Workers' Party), xv–xvi
Neurath, Otto, ix

Originary factors of production, 6
   capital as produced from, 2

Policy limitations, 89–90
Prices
   changeability of, 63, 91–94
   competitive, 38
   equilibrium, 39
   formation of, 38–39
   horizontal connectivity of, 37–90
   level of, 91–94, 101
   market and, 37–38
   original factors of production, 65–76
   production and, 91–94
   relationships, 77–78, 91–94
   role in Strigl's theory, xx–xxi
   substitution, 76
   sum of individual demands, 92
   system, 91–94
   vertical connectivity of, 37–90
Production
   adjustments, 35
   Böhm-Bawerk's views, 1, 4
   capital employment as process of, 95–96
   capital as produced means of, 2
   coordination of, 52–61
   credit expansion
      See Credit, creation
   disruption of, 11, 25, 29, 33, 35
   durable factors of, 14–26, 61
   efficiencies, 1
   factors
      substitution, 40
      supply of, 39–43
   increased, 1, 3
   innovation, 1
   interest rate allocates, 60, 109–20
   interruption by lack of subsistence fund, 7
   investment, 15–17, 23
   justified, 15
   law of returns, 46–52
   marginal productivity, 46–52, 79–90
   means of, 1–2
   momentary, 3, 17, 33
   money, 91–133
   pricing, general, 39
   process, 95–96
   roundabout methods of, 2–14
      capital constraint, 53, 67, 109
      choosing, 3, 7, 16
      credit expansion and, 115–17, 120–33
      increasing returns, 4–5, 26
      correct choice, 4–5, 7, 12, 16, 26, 32, 35, 55, 58, 60, 122–23
      interest and, 59, 96, 114
      length, 4–14, 71–72
      limits, 87–88
      reallocate, 30
      shorten, 8, 33
      structure, 21–22, 26, 85, 92–94, 102–08, 111–14
      synchronizing, 10, 14, 22–25
      technology, 86–87
      see also Capital; Savings; Wealth
Property, 93–94, 109, 114

Redistribution of property, 93–94
Reisman, George, xviiin
Renewal funds
   See Funds, renewal
Robbins, Lionel, 166–67
Robertson, D.H., 166
Röpke, Wilhelm, xii,
Roscher, Wilhelm, xxivn, 3, 28n
Rosenstein-Rodan, Paul, vii, xii
Rothbard, Murray N, xiiin, xviin, xxin, xxivn

Salerno, Joseph T., xi
Savings
    growth, 61, 65
    investments, 98, 100
Sax, Emil, xii
Say's Law, xix
Scarcity, 1
Schams, Ewald, xii
Schlesinger, Karl, xii
Schönfeld-Illy, Leon, vii, xii
Schumpeter, Joseph, ix, xii, xiii, 165
Sechrest, Larry, xxvi
Selgin, George, xxviin
Skousen, Mark, viii, xviin
Smith, Barry, vii
Spann, Othmar, x–xi
Static economy
    See Evenly rotating economy
Steindl, Joseph, ix, xvi
Strigl, Richard Ritter von
    biography and influences, vii–xvi
    method of, xx–xxii
    theory of capital, xvii–xix
Subsistence fund
    See Funds, subsistence

Taussig, Frank W., 165
Thünen, Heinrich von, 66n

Time, sacrifice of permits greater
    output, 4–6

Unemployment, 72–75

Vedder, Richard, xxin
Vertical connectivity, 37–91

Wages
    capital and, 66
    entrepreneur and, 44–45
    equilibrium, 45
    fund, 68–69, 72
    increasing production and, 72
    rates, market effect of, 69–70
    subsistence and, 68
    specific time period and, 69
Walras, Léon, xii
Wealth
    changes in, 109
    of economy, 16
    see also Money; Savings
Weiss, Franz, xii
Wicksell, Knut, xii, xviin, 57n, 165–67
Wicksteed, Philip, 52n
Wieser, Friedrich von, xi, xiii, xxivn, 30

www.ingramcontent.com/pod-product-compliance
Lightning Source LLC
Chambersburg PA
CBHW081236180526
45171CB00005B/441